GLOBALIZATION'S IMPACT ON STATE-LOCAL ECONOMIC DEVELOPMENT POLICY

GLOBALIZATION'S IMPACT ON STATE-LOCAL ECONOMIC DEVELOPMENT POLICY

CAL CLARK AND ROBERT S. MONTJOY

Nova Science Publishers, Inc.
Huntington, NY

Senior Editors: Susan Boriotti and Donna Dennis
Coordinating Editor: Tatiana Shohov
Office Manager: Annette Hellinger
Graphics: Wanda Serrano
Book Production: Matthew Kozlowski, Jonathan Rose and Jennifer Vogt
Circulation: Cathy DeGregory, Ave Maria Gonzalez, Ron Hedges and Andre Tillman

Library of Congress Cataloging-in-Publication Data

Clark, Cal, 1945-
  Globalization's impact on state-local development policy / Cal Clark and Robert S. Montjoy
    p. cm.
  Includes bibliographical references and index.
  ISBN 1-59033-017-X.
    1. United States—Economic policy—1993- 2. United States—Economic conditions—1981—
Regional disparities. 3. Globalization—Economic aspects—United States—States. I. Montjoy, Robert
S., 1944- II. Title

HC106.82 .C544 2001
338.973—dc21

                                                                                      2001045275

CONTENTS

About the Editors and Authors

Cal Clark is an Alumni Professor of Political Science at Auburn University. His major teaching and research interests focus on the political economy of development. His recent books include the co-authored *Comparing Development Patterns in Asia* and the co-edited *Beyond the Developmental State*.

Robert S. Montjoy, a Professor of Political Science, is the Assistant Vice-President for Outreach and Director of the Economic Development Institute at Auburn University. His major academic interests include economic development policy and practice. He is the co-author of *The Politics of Redistributing Urban Aid* and *The Virginia State Corporation Commission*.

Paul Brace is the Clarence L. Carter Professor of Political Science at Rice University. His research has appeared in leading political science journals. In addition to two books on the American presidency, he is the author of *State Government and Economic Performance* and co-editor of *American State and Local Politics*. At present, he is involved in a multi-year study of state supreme courts funded by the National Science Foundation.

Terry F. Buss is Professor and Chair at the Department of Public Management, Suffolk University in Boston and Visiting Fellow at the Congressional Research Service, Library of Congress in Washington, D.C. He has written widely about economic development in the US and in transitional economies.

Harry I. Chernotsky is Professor of Political Science and Director of International Studies at the University of North Carolina at Charlotte. He is currently engaged in a number of projects focusing on local responses to globalization. He is actively involved in the field of international education and has recently served as President of the Southern region of the International Studies Association.

Timothy J. Conlon is an Associate Professor of Government and Politics at George Mason University who received his Ph.D. from Harvard. He is the author of *From New Federalism to Devolution* which received the 1998 American Political Science Association's award for the best book on Federalism and Intergovernmental Relations.

Claire L. Felbinger is Chair and Professor of Public Administration at American University. Her major fields of academic interest include public works, economic development, and urban policy. She is the Editor of *Public Works Management and Policy*.

Edwin I. Gardner, Jr. is an Economic Development Officer for the city of Auburn, Alabama. He received an MPA degree from Auburn University.

Johnny Green is an Assistant Professor of Political Science at Auburn University. He has also served as a Community Renaissance Fellow in the Department of Housing and Urban Development (HUD). His major teaching and research interests are focused on the political economy of the South, economic development policy, and public administration.

Keenan Grenell is an Associate Professor of Political Science at Auburn University. His primary fields of interest include economic development policy, entrepreneurship, urban politics, and African-American politics. He has published eight articles and book chapters in these fields.

Richard Larkin is an Assistant Professor of Political Science and Planning and Acting Director of the MPA Program at the State University of West Georgia. His primary research interests include economic development and environmental policy, with a particular concern for sustainable development; and he has published four articles and numerous research reports in this area.

Kuotsai Tom Liou is an Associate Professor and Chair of Public Administration at the University of Central Florida. His recent research focuses upon economic development and administrative reform. Recent books include *Managing Economic Reforms in Post-Mao China* and *Handbook of Economic Development*.

James E. Robey is a Research Economist and Director of Regional Economic Studies at the Greater Cleveland Growth Association. His research interests include privatizing public services and functions, regional economic analysis, and rural economic development analysis.

Michelle A. Sager received a Ph.D. in Public Policy and an M.A. in International Transactions from George Mason University. She currently is a Social Science Analyst at the U.S. General Accounting Office.

Douglas J. Watson is the City Manager of Auburn, Alabama and a Visiting Professor of Political Science at Auburn University. His major areas of academic interest include economic development, local government, and urban politics. He is the author of *The New Civil War: Government Competition for Economic Development*, co-author of *The Politics of Redistributing Urban Aid*, and editor of *Innovative Governments*.

Chapter 1

THE IMPLICATIONS OF GLOBALIZATION FOR STATE-LOCAL ECONOMIC DEVELOPMENT STRATEGY

Cal Clark and Robert S. Montjoy

Over the past two decades, the growing exposure of the U.S. economy to international competition, popularly termed globalization, has brought momentous changes affecting the American economy, society, and life styles. Not surprisingly, these changes have been reflected in growing political turbulence and shifts in policy paradigms as well. This book explores the effects that globalization has had on economic development policy and practice in the United States. In the economic realm, globalization has forced a substantial change in the U.S.'s production structure. In particular, many of the nation's basic economic sectors in light and heavy industry are being forced to relocate "off shore" due to international competition; however, fortunately for the U.S., they are being replaced by a "new economy" tied to high tech industries and advanced services. Consequently, economic development policy, especially at the state and local levels where it is primarily practiced, is coming under strong challenge to respond to this industrial restructuring.

The social and economic changes associated with globalization have certainly been substantial and, in some ways, unsettling. In the 1950s and 1960s, the United States clearly had the most productive and competitive economy in the world based on techniques of the mass production of standardized goods. During the 1970s and 1980s, however, America's leading economic position came under challenge for two interconnected reasons. First, the transportation and communications revolutions made it easier to locate mass-production factories away from the existing industrial centers to take advantage of lower wages. Second, affluence made consumers increasingly eager to buy more specialized and higher quality goods than the traditional mass production techniques could fashion. By the 1990s, however, many U.S. corporations had responded quite well to this challenge, reorganizing themselves to promote high quality and high tech production and moving into advanced and sophisticated service industries. In fact, by most indices the United States has regained the lead in global competitiveness (e.g., the American unemployment rate is considerably less than Europe's and Japan has still not recovered from the long recession of the early 1990s). Still, the renewed dynamism of the U.S. economy has done little, if anything, to help many of the communities and workers who had depended upon the traditional industries for their wellbeing (Dertouzos, et al., 1989; Friedman, 1999; Gilpin, 1987; Harrison, 1994; Piore and Sabel, 1984; Thurow, 1996 & 1999; Womack, et al., 1990).

These profound changes, in turn, raise serious questions about the efficacy of state and local development policies. In the United States, the states have become increasingly active and competitive in promoting economic development, in stark contrast to the federal government's general abstinence from industrial policy (Graham, 1992). State and local economic development activities and programs span a wide gamut, although two principal types or strategies can be discerned, as summarized in Figure 1.1. The first represents the traditional strategy of attracting new investment by lowering the cost of doing business in a given locality by either subsidizing the traditional inputs used by firms (e.g., capital, land, and labor) or by limiting the "political costs" of doing business (i.e., minimizing taxes and regulation). Since these incentives were generally targeted at large mass production industries, the strategy of using them came to be called (somewhat sarcastically) "smoke-stack chasing." The other, newer strategy, which might be termed "promoting entrepreneurship," seeks to stimulate business expansion and creation by developing new markets or by providing services that enhance business operations (e.g., human capital development or support for R&D) or by offering a community with attractive amenities (Brace, 1993; Clark and Montjoy, 1998; Eisinger, 1988; Luke, et al., 1988).

An initial "wave" of state-local economic activism began in the years before World War II and continued for the first decade or so after the war. The central thrust of this wave was a drive by poorer and less industrial regions, primarily the South, to catch up with the more affluent parts of the nation; and it focused upon the conventional strategies of subsidizing business inputs and lowering political costs. The South's ability to lure industry from the Northeast and Midwest proved so successful by the 1950s that the old industrial heartland decided to fight fire with fire by emulating the South's locational incentives; and by the early 1960s the Northeast and Midwest had matched, if not surpassed, the South in incentive policies. A new wave in state and local economic development policy commenced during the 1970s and 1980s in response to the growing economic stress generated by America's shift in the global economy and by the declining amounts of federal aid. Traditional locational incentives assumed a major role in this offensive, but there was more to this wave than just the practice of economic development policy as usual. In fact, many analysts argue that a fundamental shift in strategy took place away from "smoke-stack chasing" to the much different approach of "promoting entrepreneurship," in large part because globalization was luring most of the "smoke stacks" out of the country altogether (Brace, 1993; Clark and Montjoy, 1998; Cobb, 1993; Eisinger, 1988; Kanter, 1995).

Figure 1.1: Changing Models of State-Local Economic Development Policy

Smoke-Stack Chasing	Upgrading Entrepreneurship
Theory of Growth: Growth is promoted by lowering the factor costs of production by government subsidies of capital and land and by low taxes	**Theory of Growth:** Growth is promoted by discovering, expanding, developing, or creating new markets for local goods and services
Focus of Efforts: 1. Stimulate relocation of large, established firms 2. Government supports low-risk enterprises 3. Any firm suitable target for aid	**Focus of Efforts:** 1. Stimulate new business formation and small business expansion 2. Government nurtures high-risk enterprises and activities 3. Use strategic criteria for aid
Desirable Firms: Large existing ones	**Desirable Firms:** New start-ups, small firm, high tech, environmentally friendly
Desirable Labor Force: Low-cost labor	**Desirable Labor Force:** Skilled & flexible
Primary Government Contribution: Low-cost land and tax subsidies	**Primary Government Contribution:** Access to advanced technology and finance capital
Government's Role: Government should follow and support private decisions about where to invest, what businesses will be profitable, and what producers will sell -- basically *laissez-faire*	**Government's Role:** Government should help identify investment opportunities for the private sector (i.e., new markets, products, and industries) -- movement to create public-private partnerships
Location Assets: Comparative advantage based on physical assets	**Location Assets:** Comparative advantage from social & environmental amenities
Market Focus: Local & regional	**Market Focus:** National & international

Source: Clark and Montjoy. 1998. p. 173.

This book, hence, examines globalization's impact on state and local economic development policy from two somewhat clashing perspectives. Part I charts and seeks to explain "The Expanding Global Linkages and Opportunities" of state and local governments over the last several decades. In essence, these chapters argue that the economic transformations set off by globalization are pushing state and local development policy toward fundamental change and entrepreneurial strategies that should overcome some of the problems associated with "smoke-stack chasing." Yet, caution is certainly necessary before accepting such an optimistic interpretation. Part II, therefore, presents several analyses suggesting that smoke-stack chasing "struck back" and that blind reliance on free markets and entrepreneurship can be dangerous to a community's social *and* economic health, thereby indicting the existence of "Pitfalls in a Changing Universe."

The first of four chapters in Part I by Michelle A. Sager and Timothy J. Conlan examines "The American States and Trade Promotion: Intergovernmental Cooperation Motivated by Global Competition." Chapter 2 provides a variety of data demonstrating that a tremendous increase in the "scope, scale, and sophistication" of states' international economic activities has occurred over the past two decades. Furthermore, the growing power and activism of the states in this policy realm have not come at the expense of deteriorating or conflictual relations with the federal government. Rather, very positive relations based on coordination and cooperation with the relevant federal agencies are reported. However, the recession of the early 1990s and the fiscal problems that it transmitted to many states interrupted this general growth trend and produced much more volatility in the international budgets and staffs of individual states. Sager and Conlan conclude that political leadership and business support are the most important factors driving this internationalization but that both are "two-edged swords" in the sense that many states' international efforts have also been undercut by a change in governor or by a lack of interest on the part of the small business sector that has the most to gain from help in exporting.

Chapter 3 by Kuotsai Tom Liou then provides a more detailed analysis of one central aspect of this internationalization of state economies and policies in "Foreign Direct Investment in the United States: Policy and Managerial Issues." Liou charts the very rapid rise of foreign FDI since the mid1970s and describes the international and macroeconomic conditions that have stimulated it. Liou's most striking (and, perhaps, surprising) finding, which is based on several different data sources, is that the industrial incentives offered by state and local governments have little discernible impact on foreign FDI decisions. His analysis also points to an emerging area for state policy in the need to promote cross-cultural understanding as foreign corporations assume an increasingly vital role in preserving and promoting the dynamism of many state economies.

In Chapter 4, Claire L. Felbinger and James E. Robey take a more micro look at the opportunities that globalization provides for economic upgrading with a detailed case study of "Globalization's Impact on State and Local Policy: The Rise of Regional Cluster-Based Economic Development Strategies." They contend that globalization and the rapid economic change associated with it have made long-range prediction about what industries and worker skills will emerge as "economic winners" highly problematic. Consequently, the possession of a skilled and flexible work force is becoming the key factor to attracting and keeping regional "clusters" of industries. They illustrate their analysis with a study of Cleveland's economic revitalization that was based on high tech development, regional clustering, public-private partnerships to promote development policy, and a strong emphasis on human capital development.

Part I concludes with an analysis of whether the assumed economic impacts of globalization are, in fact, occurring. According to the economic logic of globalization outlined above, it is generally assumed that the communities and states with the most developed "new economies" of high tech industries and advanced services should have the most rapidly expanding economies within the United States (or any other advanced industrial/postindustrial society). Chapter 5 on "Globalization, the 'New Economy,' and the Economic Performance of the American States" by Cal Clark and Richard Larkin tests this assumption or hypothesis with recent data on the economies of the 50 states. The analysis found that the development of a "new economy" does indeed appear to be closely tied to how well or ill a state's economy performed over the last two decades, implying that states should place increasing emphasis on the "promoting entrepreneurship" strategy of economic development.

Part I, hence, sees globalization as providing a stimulus for several positive policy transformations. However, as the old adage says, "the proof of the pudding is in the eating;" and, in fact, Part II on "Pitfalls in a Changing Universe" uncovers several significant cases of indigestion in the forms of failure to adapt fully to the emerging conditions created by globalization. Paul Brace begins Part II with Chapter 6 on "Economic Development Policy in the American States: Back to an Inglorious Future?" He finds that the "new" strategies of state and local governments to "nurture their economic strengths," which appeared to be on the upswing in the late 1980s, at least partially fell victim to the budget woes engendered by the recession of the early 1990s because their benefits were long-term while their costs were immediate. Instead, there was a return to the smoke-stack chasing hope "to lure large, trophy firms," where the benefits (new plants and jobs) come soon while most of the costs are delayed. Thus, a tremendous escalation of traditional industrial incentives occurred during the 1990s, despite the continuing lack of evidence that they have much effect on economic performance. Consequently, Brace fears that the resultant strain on the public purse will prevent the type of investments in human capital and technological infrastructure called for by the "promoting entrepreneurship" strategies for economic development.

Two detailed case studies of responses to globalization then give a more nuanced picture of state and local governments simultaneously responding both well and poorly to the challenges and opportunities of globalization. Chapter 7 by Douglas J. Watson, Edwin I. Gardner, Jr., and Robert S. Montjoy presents a detailed case study of one of the most lucrative sets of industrial incentives ever extended in "Moving into Global Competition: A Case Study of Alabama's Recruitment of Mercedes-Benz." This study gives more than a little support to Brace's arguments since Alabama's triumph was soon followed by a public relations and political debacle when various parts of the Alabama offer became public. Yet, a half decade later, the state appears to have benefitted from the

Mercedes recruitment; and, most significantly, the successful recruitment of a series of high-wage industries has required far less in state concessions. Consequently, it is certainly possible to argue that the incentives offered by Alabama represented very expensive "table stakes" that have enabled the state to enter a clearly higher level of the new global game of economic development.

Harry I. Chernotsky then moves the level of analysis to the city in "Charlotte's Response Globalization: The Mayor's International Cabinet" in Chapter 8. He attributes the tremendous increase that has occurred in cities' international activities to a combination of three factors: 1) the growing importance of international economic linkages for them, 2) the federal withdrawal from urban policy during the Reagan era, and 3) the growing professionalization and entrepreneurship of city administrators. He is particularly interested in the changes in institutional structure that are required to increase a city's capacity for global involvement and uses a case study of the Mayor's International Cabinet in Charlotte to illustrate the importance of such factors as mayoral leadership and the development of public-private partnerships. However, his analysis also illustrates the fragility of such new bodies as well since the fate of the Cabinet turned out to ride to a considerable extent on the whims of a changing set of political leaders.

Chapter 9 on "Recapturing the Future? The Implications of Globalization for Education and Entrepreneurship in U.S. Economic Development Strategies" by Cal Clark, Johnny Green, and Keenan Grenell argues that the current dynamics in the U.S. political economy are pushing state-local development policies in contradictory directions. On the one hand, America's transformation from the Industrial Age to the Information Age implies that state and local development strategies need to be reoriented to emphasize education and entrepreneurship, two factors that spurred America's early industrialization in the late nineteenth and early twentieth centuries. Yet, the current practice of economic development that seeks to provide massive subsidies to business denies state government the resources needed for transforming their economic development policies, thereby creating a policy paradox that can only be transcended by bridging the normal cleavages between conservatives and liberals in contemporary American politics.

Finally, Chapter 10 on "Exporting American Economic Development Practice to Russia" by Terry F. Buss critiques the state-and-local response to globalization from another, very different perspective. Buss describes how attempts to export (i.e., replicate) the American model of local economic development to Russia generally failed because of the much different set of institutions there (i.e., lack of legal support for a market, rampant corruption and mafia control of the economy, an extractive state bureaucracy, and so forth). This shows that blind reliance on the market to solve economic problems does not appear warranted. Market competition provides perverse incentives in the United States as well. For example, businesses demand a high quality labor force. Yet, they use the "new civil war" among the states to gain large tax abatements, often affecting the local taxes that fund education. Clearly, something does not add up!

To sum, the implications of the changing economic realities brought on by globalization for state and local economic development efforts are complex. First, barring major policy change at the national level, states will be forced to compete increasingly hard to attract and retain industries. Second, the impetus this provides for cutting taxes and public services is severely limited by the needs of corporations for a skilled and flexible work force to stay viable in an advanced industrial nation. That is, the old Southern strategy of accentuating the characteristics of a Third World economy is almost certainly doomed to failure. Third, the importance of attracting new businesses is not just for the new jobs that they directly bring. Rather, the access that they can provide local businesses to world-wide corporate networks may be just as vital for regenerating economic growth. Finally, education is clearly an important area in several regards: 1) basic literacy and math training in primary and secondary schools; 2) specific skills that a particular business needs that vo-tech and community colleges can provide; and 3) partnerships between research universities and high tech firms. Taken together, these somewhat contradictory trends imply that economic development policy at the state and local level is just beginning a long journey and transformation.

REFERENCES

Brace, P. 1993. *State Government and Economic Performance*. Baltimore: Johns Hopkins University Press.

Clark, C. and R. Montjoy. 1998. "Globalization and the Revitalization of U.S. Economic Competitiveness: Implications for Economic Development Policy," pp. 151-182 in K.T. Liou, Ed. *Handbook of Economic Development*. New York: Marcel Dekker.

Cobb, J.C. 1993. *The Selling of the South: The Southern Crusade for Industrial Development, 1936-1990*. Urbana: University of Illinois Press.

Dertouzos, M.L., R.K. Lester, and R.M. Solow. 1989. *Made in America: Regaining the Productive Edge*. Cambridge: MIT Press.

Eisinger, P.K. 1988. *The Rise of the Entrepreneurial State: State and Local Economic Development Policy in the United States*. Madison: University of Wisconsin Press.

Friedman, T.L. 1999. *The Lexus and the Olive Tree*. New York: Farrar, Strauss, Giroux.

Gilpin, R. 1987. *The Political Economy of International Relations*. Princeton: Princeton University Press.

Graham, O.L., Jr. 1992. *Losing Time: The Industrial Policy Debate*. Cambridge: Harvard University Press.

Harrison, B. 1994. *Lean and Mean: The Changing Landscape of Corporate Power in the Age of Flexibility*. New York: Basic Books.

Kanter, R.M. 1995. *World Class: Thriving Locally in the Global Economy*. New York: Simon & Schuster.

Luke, J.S., C. Ventriss, B.J. Reed, and C.M. Reed. 1988. *Managing Economic Development: A Guide to State and Local Leadership Strategies*. San Francisco: Jossey-Bass.

Piore, M.J. and C.F. Sabel. 1984. *The Second Industrial Divide: Possibilities for Prosperity*. New York: Basic Books.

Thurow, L.C. 1996. *The Future of Capitalism: How Today's Economic Forces Shape Tomorrow's World*. New York: Morrow.

Thurow, L.C. 1999. *Building Wealth: The New Rules for Individuals, Companies, and Nations in a Knowledge-Based Economy*. New York: HarperCollins.

Womack, J.P., D.T. Jones, and D. Roos. 1990. *The Machine that Changed the World: The Story of Lean Production*. New York: Macmillan.

I. EXPANDING GLOBAL LINKAGES AND OPPORTUNITIES

Chapter 2

THE AMERICAN STATES AND TRADE PROMOTION: INTERGOVERNMENTAL COOPERATION MOTIVATED BY GLOBAL COMPETITION

Michelle A. Sager and Timothy J. Conlan

At the dawn of the 21st century, American policy makers face new challenges as they respond to the end of the Cold War, the pressures of a global economy, and rapid social and technological change. Internationally, the bipolar competition of the Cold War era has given way to a complex new environment shaped by new issues of global interdependence and economic restructuring. Domestically, the balance of power and responsibilities between the federal government and the states is shifting downward as federal discretionary spending falls, the government's civilian employment declines, and the national policy agenda becomes increasingly constrained. In contrast, state governments in the U.S. have entered a new era of activism and innovation (Fosler, 1988; Kincaid, 1990; Kline, 1983). Their governing institutions have been modernized, their finances broadened, their staffs professionalized, and their legislatures made more representative of all their citizens.

How are these newly empowered states responding to the emerging global environment? What new international activities are states initiating? Is there a broad-gauged trend affecting all states or one centered on a few internationally-oriented jurisdictions? To what extent is there a new dimension of international relations developing? If this new dimension is significant, what are its implications for state economic development policy?

This chapter explores these questions by examining the international activities of state governments. Based on telephone and personal interviews with 95 state, local and federal officials in 25 states (for a list of all 25, see Figure 2.8 (p.29)), site visits to five states, and the synthesis and analysis of data collected by the National Association of State Development Agencies (NASDA), the study provides an analytical overview of state-supported international activities and the implications of these findings for economic development (Conlan and Sager, 1997 discuss these issues in much more detail).

THE CONTEXT OF STATE INTERNATIONAL ACTIVITIES

The nation state has been the central actor in international relations for more than 200 years. Yet, in recent years, the "demise" of the nation state has been predicted with increasing frequency as country after country faces new challenges from without and within (Latouche, 1998; Matthews, 1997). On the one hand, existing nations are too small to deal individually with a growing list of global problems. At the same time, many are too large to accommodate internal demands for greater regional autonomy and local self-governance. For example, resource and environmental problems that once could be addressed locally or nationally now require solutions on an international scale. From ocean fisheries to atmospheric ozone, nations are obliged to enter into international treaties to deal with what have become global problems. Similarly, on trade and economic issues, many nations are ceding power and authority to new supranational institutions, such as the World Trade Organization and the European Union, and are entering expansive regional trade agreements, such as NAFTA. To be sure, predictions of the nation state's demise can be exaggerated (Slaughter, 1997). Nation states remain the principal actors on the world stage (Henkin, 1996); they continue to be the chief participants on international issues from economic trade to armed defense; but changes are underway. Nation states have lost their previous monopoly over many international issues -- both political and economic -- as power has been formally delegated to (or informally seeped toward) a broad range of other institutions: supranational organizations, multinational corporations, and -- most importantly for this study -- subnational entities: states, provinces, cities, and regional collaborations (Fry, 1998).

The past twenty years have seen dramatic growth in the international activities of state governments. This has been most apparent in the areas of trade promotion and economic development, where states have been responding to an increasingly global economy (Archer and Maser, 1989). Although states as a whole have become increasingly active in promoting their economies on an international scale, the degree of activity varies considerably from state to state (Cavusgil and Czinkota, 1990). The states surveyed for this report generally fall into three broad categories. First, large states, as well as those with a particularly strong commitment to international activity, face unique challenges in priority setting and program organization. For example, California, Minnesota and New York have all confronted the need to coordinate diverse activities and innovations across functions and to focus on those activities which have proven most effective. The use of more sophisticated performance measures, identification of key industry sectors or clusters, and fee-based services are a few of the responses developed by these states.

Most states fall into a second category of moderate size and activity. These states tend to provide many of the same core services as those above; and many have begun to branch out from trade promotion into other functional areas (whether by accident or strategic planning). They frequently must defend continued funding in order to gain legislative approval. Funding constraints have resulted in innovative partnerships with the private sector, have encouraged leveraging of federal funds, and have stimulated partnerships with other state agencies and universities. Third, a final tier of states generally includes the smallest in terms of both population and budget. For these states, the primary challenge is to maintain a base level of international operations (including a viable international trade office and overseas representation) in the face of tight budgets and/or a lack of enthusiasm for exporting on the part of businesses or the legislature. These states tend to provide limited services and often find that their services are reactive rather than strategic.

TRADE AND ECONOMIC DEVELOPMENT

Over the past 20 years, states on the whole have greatly expanded their internationally-focused economic development activities. Most now offer a range of services to assist businesses seeking to develop or expand export markets, and many work hard to attract foreign investment from abroad. The average state now supports four foreign trade offices abroad and a staff of eleven at home (National Association of State Development Agencies, 1994). These averages obscure substantial variations among the states in their international activities, however. They also fail to reflect the considerable volatility that exists in state funding and staffing of international activities.

Growth Trends in Trade Activity

The U.S. states have always been active promoters of their local economies (Scheiber, 1993). These state powers were once focused almost exclusively on the domestic economy. When states looked outside their borders for economic opportunities, it tended to be regarded as "smoke-stack chasing" -- the recruitment of industry, jobs, and investment from other jurisdictions. Yet, as Figure 2.1 demonstrates, the United States has been inexorably growing more internationalized over the past several decades in terms of the importance of both exports and imports for the its national economy.

This economic change, in turn, stimulated the states to move in a new direction with their economic development programs. Consequently, by the 1980s many states had responded with remarkable swiftness to the growing internationalization of the economy. In 1969, only four states had established even a single overseas office to promote the sale of goods and services produced within their borders. By 1984, there were 56 state overseas offices; and more states had opened offices in other countries than had established offices in Washington, D.C. (Scheiber, 1993). Over the next decade, as graphed in Figure 2.2, the number of overseas offices and the personnel staffing them more than doubled. In 1994, for instance, there were 162 state offices abroad, and the average state had more than three foreign offices. The growth of staff almost exactly paralleled that of overseas offices, jumping from 400 in 1984 to 900 ten years later (National Association of State Development Agencies, 1994).

**Figure 2.1: Internationalizing the U.S. Economy Imports
and Exports as a Percent of GDP, 1970-1999**

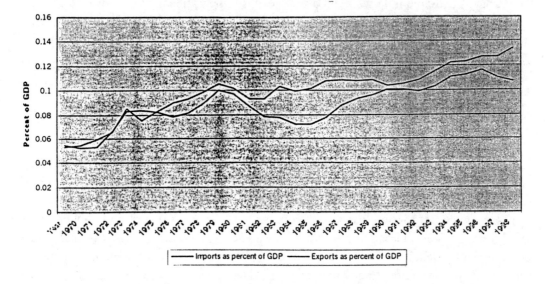

Figure 2.2: International Trade Activities of State Governments, 1982-1994

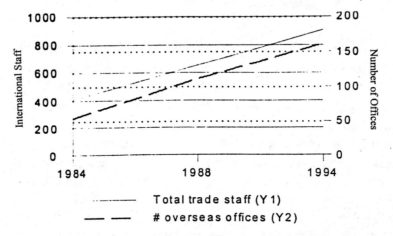

Measured in current dollars, total state spending on international trade activities grew even more rapidly in the 1980s than staff or overseas offices, jumping by three-and-a-half fold between 1982 and 1990 from slightly under $20 million to slightly over $70 million (see Figure 2.3). Spending growth leveled off in the early 1990s, however, as state revenues stagnated during a period of recession and state expenditures were squeezed by the rapid growth of spending on Medicaid and corrections (National Association of State Development Agencies, 1994). Finally, the regional focus of states' overseas activities has shifted even as it has grown, adapting to changes in the world economy. Whereas states originally focused their overseas offices in Europe, by the mid 1990s they had shifted their emphasis to East Asia. Japan had become the most popular destination, and it was joined in the top five by Mexico, Taiwan, Germany, and Korea.

Figure 2.3: Combined State Spending on International Activities, 1982-1996

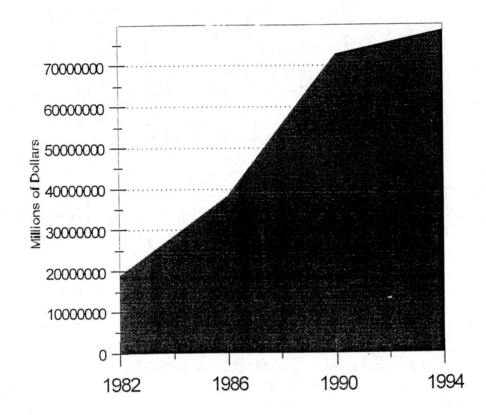

Volatility in International Programs

The general growth patterns in state international budgets and staffing obscure significant variations from state to state and from year to year. Thus, while combined state spending on international activities inched upwards in the early 1990s, as indicated in Figure 2.4, international trade and development budgets in a number of states were actually being reduced during this period of fiscal stress. For example, California, which was hit particularly hard by the 1991 recession, cut its budget for international trade activities almost in half between 1990 and 1994. Deep spending cuts were also made by Virginia and Washington during this four year span. On the other hand, spending on trade activities increased during this period in New York and New Mexico. Thus, the overall growth in state international spending between 1982 and 1994 obscured considerable volatility -- both up and down -- within individual state budgets during this same period.

Figure 2.4: International Trade Budgets in Selected States, 1982-1994

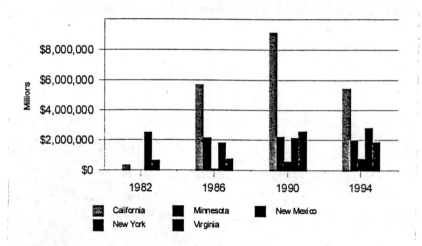

Such volatility has been apparent in good times as well as bad. For example, Empire State Development, the economic development agency of New York, conducted a survey of state overseas activity in 1997. In the three short years from 1994 to 1997, the study found that states had opened a net total of 26 new trade offices abroad, raising the total number to 191. But this overall increase hid a great deal of additional change. A grand total of 71 new state trade offices were opened abroad during this three year period, with the largest number occurring in South America. At the same time, 28 other offices were closed. Connecticut alone closed seven offices (most of them in China or Mexico), while opening three new ones in South America and Korea. Mississippi closed four offices and opened three. Texas closed three foreign offices. Thus, rapid change and adaptation to new markets remains the order of the day.

Interstate Disparities

A great deal of variation occurs from state to state, as well as over time. States differ considerably from one another -- in terms of population, wealth, and governmental spending -- and their international activities reflect these differences. For example, in 1998 the average international trade budget for the 10 most populous U.S. states was $3,874,895. For the ten least populous states, the average was well under one-tenth that amount, or $278,899. Similarly, the ten largest states employed, on average, a staff of 15 domestic and overseas personnel in their trade divisions in 1994. The ten smallest states, in contrast, had an average staff of only four.

Not surprisingly, this pattern affected overseas activities as well. The ten most populous states had an average of 5.5 overseas offices in 1994 to assist in the development of export markets and the attraction of foreign investment. The ten least populous states averaged less than one office apiece. While six mostly small states had no overseas offices at all in 1998, large states like Pennsylvania, Ohio, California, and New

York had offices in nine to fifteen different countries. In fact, only the very largest states have the resources for investing in international economic activities. Figure 2.5, for example, shows that while the size of a state's budget in this area is strongly correlated with its population, the top quintile on population (8 states) has a disproportionately huge advantage, spending over three times as much on average than the states in even the fourth quintile. These disparities, though, were not for want of trying on the part of most smaller states. On a per capita basis, the least populous states spent almost as much as their larger counterparts. The smallest states spent an average of $.28 per capita on international trade activities in 1998, compared to $.29 by the ten largest states (Conway and Nothdurft, 1996).

Figure 2.5: 1998 State Trade Budgets by Population

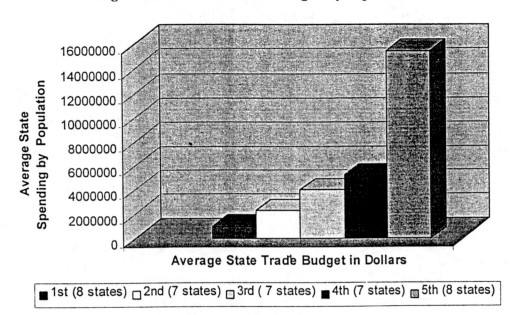

States also vary in the scope and range of services they provide in the international trade arena. Unlike budget size and staffing levels, these variations do not correlate strongly with state population. All states that are active in trade and export promotion attempt to provide a range of services to their clients, although the precise mix of services varies from state to state. Detailed case studies of state activities make clear, however, that the level of state resources does affect the quality and intensity of state services. Virtually all states (including Puerto Rico and the Virgin Islands) provide in-house counseling to potential exporters. Similarly, 48 states provide market research services. Most states also hold "how-to-export" conferences and seminars, operate trade promotion programs, provide support for trade shows, and organize trade missions. However, fewer than half of the states provide trade development training or have established a gubernatorial-level international advisory council.

STATE ECONOMIC PROMOTION IN OTHER FUNCTIONAL AREAS

Trade and investment policies are the natural focal points of state activities to promote their local economies, and they are the areas of most concerted state activity. Economic goals are increasingly pursued in other functional areas as well, though, as states grope toward enhancing their international presence. Agriculture, for example, is a major component of the U.S. economy, and the patterns of state activity in promoting agricultural products worldwide bear close resemblance to state actions promoting export trade in general. International economic development activities involving education and environmental protection are more distinctive. These tend to be nascent and developing fields for most states, with a rich but uneven mixture of state level initiatives and diverse partnerships with federal programs and other state initiatives.

Agriculture

Agriculture is a major industry in many states, and several have sophisticated and well established international operations. Among the states sampled in this report, Departments of Agriculture in eight states have their own international trade divisions or offices. In at least five states (Georgia, Idaho, Illinois, Kentucky, and Missouri), Departments of Agriculture share financing and use of joint overseas trade offices. In other cases, Agriculture Department officials operate their own overseas offices.

State international activities in agriculture have greatly benefitted from long-term cooperative relationships with the federal government. This federal-state cooperation operates on many levels, including agricultural research, education, dissemination, and export financing and assistance. For example, the U.S.D.A.'s Foreign Agricultural Service (FAS) provides substantial funding that helps support state export and marketing programs. According to one Minnesota agricultural trade official, mutual benefits flow from federal-state cooperation: "We do a lot with FAS. They need our local contacts, and we need their worldwide contacts." Some of the FAS funding is channeled through a series of regional, multi-state Agricultural Trade Assistance programs (including EUSAFEC, MIATCO, SUSTA, and WUSATA) that work effectively with many individual states.

Agriculture is also the field that tends to be most closely coordinated with state economic development trade offices. There are many examples of such cooperation besides the sharing of overseas facilities mentioned earlier. In Indiana, the Commissioner of Agriculture's office helps to support an agricultural trade specialist housed in the Commerce Department's international trade office. In Minnesota, the International Trade Office began as a unit inside the state Department of Agriculture before it became an independent entity.

Because of the long history of governmental involvement in agriculture and the high level of state-federal cooperation, small rural states have developed the most elaborate strategies for coping with resource limitations in this field. For example, New Mexico's state Department of Agriculture is physically located at New Mexico State University --

the state's land grant college, 300 miles from the state capitol. There it is able to combine state resources supporting both agriculture and education with federal research and educational assistance. Agricultural extension agents at the university help staff the department's marketing efforts in Mexico. While there, they also help recruit Mexican students to attend the university. Using its educational base, the Department also hires graduate students in agriculture from East Asian universities to staff its overseas offices in Singapore and Tokyo.

Environmental Protection

Environmental regulation has become an important domestic policy focus for state governments. Increasingly, states are discovering that environmental protection has international implications as well. Several states -- often with assistance from the USAEP and other federal agencies -- have begun promoting commercial export applications of environmental technologies to industrializing nations in Asia and elsewhere. Of the states sampled in this study, environmental export and technology transfer programs had been completed or were underway in at least nine states. Colorado, for example, is participating in the Department of Energy's Ambassadors program which provides support for foreign environmental professionals to visit with Colorado environmental companies in hopes of generating new business. In Maine, the governor and the Department of Economic Development have identified environmental services and products as the state's number one international growth area. As a result, the Maine Department of Environmental Protection is "becoming a kind of trade representative for Maine's environmental research and product market. This is a huge growth area, and our international activities are just starting out." The Department is seeking ways to export entire projects. For example, "if a developing country needed a sewage plant, we would provide the plant, the regulatory infrastructure, and people to help set up that infrastructure."

With its strong environmental track record and advanced environmental technology industry, California may be farthest along in implementing this kind of commercial vision. CalEPA and the state's Trade and Commerce Agency have established a joint program, the California Technical Environmental Partnership, and have been promoting environmental technology overseas for three years. As the managing director of the Partnership put it:

> We want to try to capture some of the costs it took to meet our environmental standards. Environmental technology exports help us do it. It creates jobs, strengthens the environmental industry, promotes trade, fosters diplomacy, and helps clean up the environment in foreign countries. The market for environmental technology in Asia is expanding rapidly. The potential there is huge.

Education

International activities in education typically conjure up visions of exchange programs. Educational exchanges are important, but state-related international initiatives in education go well beyond exchange programs. They include varied programs designed to enlist the resources of state educational institutions in support of international economic development opportunities. To date, such programs are mostly small and have evolved haphazardly. As one New York trade official put it: "The universities are a great resource for relationships, but they have taken a helter-skelter approach [to international activities]."

One of the most widely established initiatives is the Small Business Development Centers (SBDC) program sponsored by the Small Business Administration. In the vast majority of states, these centers are housed at and administered by state educational institutions -- universities, colleges, or community colleges. They are intended to provide "one-stop shopping" for assistance and training services to small businesses. While the program as a whole is not focused on international trade, individual SBDCs emphasize or provide international export training. For example, approximately 10 percent of the clients at Albuquerque's SBDC seek export assistance.

Other examples of education-trade alliances abound across the states. The range of alliances is remarkable. California has established a network of nine Centers for International Trade Development within the state's community college system. These centers are jointly funded by the state Chancellor's office and the participating colleges. As the state program director explained in an interview:

> We assist small businesses to enter the international market or increase their market share. We also work with colleges, faculty and students to help globalize their curriculum. We are starting to see some overlap and duplication of services as more SBDCs are funded by [the Department of] Trade and Commerce, but we do different stuff. The key is to coordinate niches, to not be territorial.

In Illinois, the International Trade Division coordinates a statewide network of trade centers that are located at universities or community colleges. Universities in New York and Virginia have developed programs that allow MBA students to perform market research for international trade ventures. Finally, many states rely on university students, faculty, and alumni to help provide foreign business contacts. As the director of Maryland's Office of International Business observed: "The universities have an array of experts, students, and contracts that provide contacts for this office." This concept of utilizing foreign students and alumni to establish business contacts overseas has been formalized in Washington state, where legislation was passed in 1996 establishing an "international contact database" for such connections *(Clearinghouse,* 1996: 1).

FACTORS PROMOTING AND INHIBITING STATE INTERNATIONAL ACTIVITIES

What forces have led states into the international arena? What factors have restrained them from becoming as active as they might like to be? This study's survey of state, federal, and local government officials identified several factors on both sides of the equation which are recorded in Figure 2.6. Some are double-edged swords. For example, strong political leadership was commonly cited in interviews as a source of inspiration for state international initiatives. But a change of political leadership can rapidly alter such commitments and redirect priorities toward a different set of policy goals. This is most evident in budgetary decisions. As indicated earlier, the rapid growth of state international trade budgets in the 1980s has been replaced in many states with reductions, stagnation, or budget instability through much of the 1990s. The resulting fiscal problems were the most frequently mentioned constraint on state international activities today.

Figure 2.6: Principal Constraints on State International Trade Offices

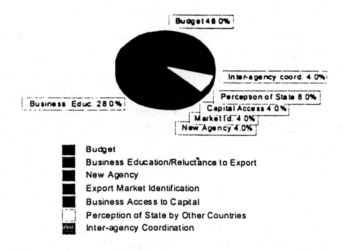

Even the business community can play dual roles in the eyes of survey respondents. Current or potential exporters and investors are the most important constituencies for many of these state programs; and the private sector's commitment to a global economy was often identified as a compelling factor in stimulating government policies in this area. Yet, a lack of business awareness of export opportunities, especially among the small and medium sized businesses that are the primary clientele of export oriented programs, was a commonly cited constraint as well. Overall, each of these factors is important, and each deserves attention in some detail.

Leadership

Political leadership was singled out as a factor promoting state international involvement by survey respondents in multiple states. Although leadership can come from both the legislative and executive branches of government, governors were mentioned far more often than state legislatures in this regard. Thus, Indiana officials pointed to the role played by a "series of supportive governors." A western state respondent stressed that a recent governor "pushed foreign trade hard in his second term." A federal official in Minnesota drew attention to the role of Governor Perpich in the 1980s, who made international trade an important plank in his first election campaign. Only in the states of Alaska and California was comparable attention drawn to the contributions of the state legislature.

Gubernatorial attention to an international agenda, particularly in the area of trade promotion, is not surprising. Economic growth is a goal most policy makers espouse. In an increasingly global economy, promoting export trade and attracting foreign investment fit naturally into this posture. "The primary motivation for our international activities is increasing economic development," said one state trade official. "Job creation was the motivation," said another. "Export-related jobs pay more."

But while international economic programs may bask in the sunshine of one particular administration, they may be relegated to the shadows in the next. Thus, some international programs experienced difficulties when a new governor gained election with a different, domestically-focused, set of priorities. One respondent suggested, perhaps apocryphally, that an earlier governor "didn't even have a passport in his first term." Another remarked that the current governor "couldn't care less" about international trade. To make matters worse, he said that the governor was reluctant to accompany foreign trade missions because "he's concerned about bad press." Another trade official decried the lack of any "long term legislative commitment" to international activities. In short, the loss or absence of high-level political commitment to international activities was one of the most commonly expressed obstacles to state activity in this field.

Resources

Political transitions help to explain the pattern of on-again, off-again funding that many state international trade and investment programs have experienced. For example, Figure 2.7 shows the percent change in state international appropriations from FY 1992 to FY 1994. Twenty-one states experienced spending cuts -- ranging from 2 percent to 71 percent of their 1992 budgets, while twenty-two states had budget increases of 1 percent to 446 percent. More importantly, 17 states -- or one-third of the total for which data were available -- had appropriation increases or decreases exceeding 25 percent in a single two-year period.

This cycle of budgetary feast and famine was identified as a major problem by officials in a plurality of states. Successful international relationships -- in trade and elsewhere -- often begin slowly and require a foundation of trust and stability. For new activities, there are start-up costs and learning curves. Whether they resulted from fiscal volatility or from consistently low levels of investment, in contrast, the resulting budget constraints were the most commonly cited obstacle to successful international programs. Shrinking budgets were especially troublesome for some states, forcing cutbacks in travel, the closing of offices, and/or the layoff of personnel. In other cases, serious constraints were imposed by funding levels that failed to keep up with growing demands. "Big budgets and big staffs are gone," said one administrator from a Midwestern state. "Our budget has been flat for five years, but exports have doubled and our trade shows and missions doubled. In the future we'll find that we can't serve everybody."

Figure 2.7: Percent Change in State International Appropriations, 1992-1994

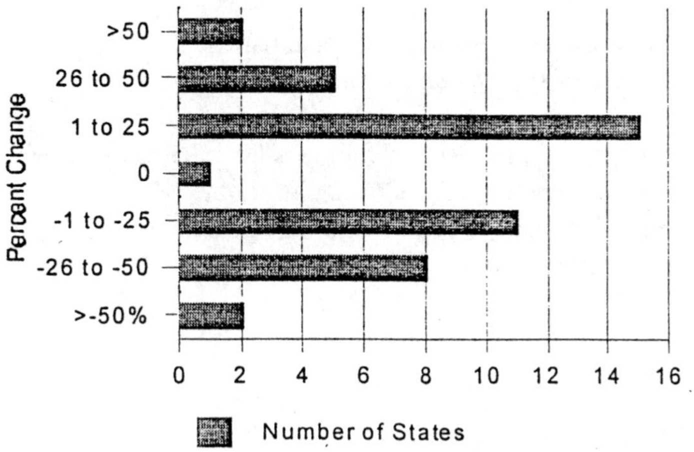

The Political Environment

The political environment operating within states also plays an important role shaping their international activities. A general recognition of global economic change was one commonly mentioned factor leading to greater state involvement abroad. "International trade is becoming more and more important to the state economy," observed one Midwestern trade official. "Oregon's proximity to Southeast Asia and the NICs" strongly shaped that state's approach, according to another state official. Such general perceptions of economic trends and potential competitive advantages often translate directly into support for international trade promotion activities from a state's business community. Many state officials identified business support as an important factor promoting state involvement in overseas development activities. "Globalization is here, and companies are beginning to realize their competition is from all over the world," observed an Indiana trade department official. "The business community is a big promoter of our international activities," explained a legislative staffer in another state.

At the same time, many state trade officials suggested that private sector attitudes posed challenges, as well. This was especially true of small and medium sized firms, which tended to be the principal clients of trade promotion activities. After budget constraints, state trade officials identified a lack of international awareness within the business community, along with a corresponding reluctance to explore export opportunities, as the most common obstacles they faced. As one Midwestern official put it: "The greatest challenge is getting companies to look at exporting. There are 20,000 manufacturers in Illinois, and the majority do not export. It's difficult to get management to commit the resources needed to begin exporting." A trade specialist from a neighboring state agreed: "The greatest challenge has been trying to increase awareness for international business."

THE BENEFITS OF STATE INTERNATIONAL ACTIVITIES

Multiple benefits can be attributed to the international activities of state governments. Economic benefits are most commonly claimed. Unfortunately, while agency outputs are easily measured (the number of trade missions organized or trade leads referred, for example), actual impacts on the economy are much harder to pin down. However, other beneficial but non-economic impacts often get lost in the debate over outcome measures. These include the promotion of international understanding, greater intergovernmental cooperation, environmental enhancements, and opportunities for policy innovation.

Economic Benefits

The most common justification for state international economic activity is that it pays off in increased foreign trade, investment, and job creation. Positive economic effects are generally inferred from indicators of agency activity: the number of trade leads generated, referrals made, inquiries answered, seminars conducted, trade missions organized, and so forth. For example, the director of Washington state's trade office prepares a quarterly report itemizing a standard set of "measurable results," including the number of business clients served, client counseling hours, trade shows attended, incoming and outgoing trade missions, presentations made, and training seminars organized. In some cases, activity measures may be linked explicitly to a variety of favorable economic outcomes, such as an expanding volume of exports, an increase in export-related jobs, or the attraction of new foreign investment. Thus, one state trade office director reported that "our accomplishments include increased attendance at trade shows and a tremendous increase in wood product exports." Another bragged that, "We estimate that we are responsible for about 15 percent of total exports, and then we transpose this into jobs. That's what the legislature cares about. We estimate 23 jobs are created for every $1 million in exports, so we created 22,330 jobs in 1996."

Such economic claims are difficult to substantiate, however. There has clearly been a correlation between expanding state international trade activities and U.S. export growth. As shown earlier in Figure 2.1, exports of U.S. goods and services have risen steadily since 1970, in tandem with state export promotion budgets. Attributing export growth to state activities is another matter, however. There have been many other economic and policy developments during this period that may have been responsible for the increase in exports. Experiments cannot be staged to test which factors may have been most important or what would have happened in the absence of state promotional activities.

Consequently, many trade officials are uncomfortable with making precise economic claims for their programs; and several disavowed even trying to do so. "There is no tangible way to measure the impact of export promotion," one official stated. The Deputy Director of Indiana's International Trade Division expressed a similar position in detail:

> The sorts of accomplishments generated by these international activities depend on how you look at it. In the aggregate, exports in Indiana tripled in eight years. However, the overall environment for exports was good, and the question is whether the increase can be attributed to our office. For us to say we are responsible for export dollar figures is a bit salacious. The government doesn't create exports, so we don't hang our hat on the number of dollars generated. Our office does generate finite data on the number of companies worked with, dollars in sales achieved, contracts signed, trade leads generated, etc.

Nonetheless, it is plausible to infer that a positive relationship exists among state export promotion activity, the volume of exports, and jobs. Evidence for such a linkage is suggested by the experience of agriculture. Agriculture accounts for approximately half of all U.S. exports, but it comprises only about one-tenth of the total U.S. economy. Although there are various explanations for this, it is noteworthy that combined federal and state spending on behalf of agricultural exports far exceeds that for other economic sectors.

Even positive cost-benefit analyses are no guarantee that programs will be funded, however. Agricultural export programs, for example, have been attacked in Congress as wasteful examples of "corporate welfare;" and the response is often the same at the state level. Washington state's Local Trade Assistance Network (LTAN) program was a rural export promotion program jointly sponsored by the state Departments of Trade and Agriculture. Evaluations found that the program met most of its goals and generated more than enough growth-related tax revenues to cover its costs. But the program was terminated by the Legislature regardless, due in part to the constraints imposed by state expenditure limits.

Non-Economic Benefits

Often lost in the debate over economic performance measures are the non-economic benefits that can accrue from state international activities. These include: 1) contributions to U.S. foreign policy, including the promotion of international understanding; 2) environmental accomplishments, including the transfer of *institutional* as well as physical technology; and 3) policy innovations, including the diffusion of new techniques of effective governance. Above all, state international activities can play an important role in broadening and deepening America's connections with the world at large. Although such non-economic benefits are even more difficult to quantify than commercial benefits, their value can be just as significant.

One of the most important consequences of state international involvement is the capacity to contribute to broader U.S. foreign policy interests, including the promotion of international understanding and goodwill. This is the principal goal of the growing number of sister city and sister state relationships that have proliferated in recent years. The same is true of traditional educational exchange programs. Newer, still evolving federal-state programs, which begin with other goals in mind, may become increasingly important from a foreign policy perspective. For example, the Minnesota Pollution Control Agency, with support from the USAEP, undertook a waste management project in the Phillippines. According to the project's director, one of the venture's principal spinoffs has been "promoting friendship between countries."

Apart from contributing toward broader foreign policy objectives, states have much to offer other countries in the realm of policy advice and institutional technology. States are often better equipped than the federal government to offer tangible assistance to foreign governments. They are closer to many of the problems, more actively engaged in operational issues and problem solving, and more comparable in scale to many of the nations needing assistance. In environmental policy, for example, the federal government promulgates broad regulatory policies and standards in the areas of air and water pollution, drinking water, toxic chemicals, and hazardous waste disposal. State and local governments shoulder most of the responsibility for implementing policies and standards, monitoring behavior, enforcing regulations, and operating public facilities. Accordingly, state and local government officials often have acquired a great deal of unique operational experience that may be of great value to other countries embarking on programs of pollution prevention, reduction, and mitigation. As one state official observed:

> Maine has a lot to offer other countries. Our companies usually offer products and services at a lower cost. They also have a lot of remote land they have developed, so they have done the "problem solving" that developing countries might find useful. And finally, the state has tough environmental laws, so they have to meet a lot of challenges.

Finally, state and local involvement in international affairs can also promote the diffusion of specific policy ideas and solutions among nations. Interviews with state and local officials uncovered several examples of this. Officials from India, on a mission to New Mexico, acquired concrete ideas for improving their wastewater treatment facilities in arid regions. California State University, Sacramento has been active in providing technical assistance to states from the former Soviet Union. For example, the university trained officials from the Ministry of Finance in Turkmenistan in tax collection techniques and then had them intern at the California Franchise Tax Board. The city of Chattanooga, Tennessee has pioneered sustainable development and pollution prevention technologies and has been active in promoting these approaches worldwide.

The diffusion of policy innovations is a two-way street, however, and internationally-active jurisdictions have much to gain from other countries in return. In the field of environmental protection, for example, an official with the Council of State Governments emphasized the value of this "two-way flow of information:"

Many Asian governments have close relationships with the private sector. Seeing this at work in the environmental sector was eye-opening. It's very different from the adversarial system in the U.S. Success stories from Asia, where the public and private sectors work together, can provide lessons for this country.

Precisely this kind of lesson was acquired in Minnesota, as a result of participation in a CSG/US-AEP waste management project in the Philippines. The project director noted that her agency, the Minnesota Pollution Control Agency, had "never worked with businesses before; we had only regulated them." Minnesota businesses involved in the project "now have a different view of the MPCA. They view the relationship as a partnership instead of just command and control."

COOPERATION AND CONFLICT IN
STATE INTERNATIONAL ACTIVITIES

This study found patterns of intergovernmental and inter-state cooperation in state efforts to address the demands of the global economy through state international trade offices. There was a great deal of mixing and sharing of responsibilities between the different levels of government, and relationships were typically friendly and supportive. In addition, state officials cooperate with their counterparts in other states in order to maximize their resources. In the case of export promotion, state officials often used terms like "excellent" and "wonderful" to describe federal-state relations, and these views were generally shared by federal agency employees. Similarly, none of the state officials interviewed for this study characterized their relationships with other states as conflictual or even competitive.

Clearly, it is much easier for two parties to work together if they are seeking the same result. In the case of state and local involvement in international affairs, federal, state, and local officials are most likely to agree when they are seeking to improve the economy. This is a goal that is almost universally supported. Although disagreements can occur over the proper approach to achieve this goal, such disagreements tend not to occur vertically -- between federal and state officials -- but horizontally -- between state or local jurisdictions competing to attract new investment or between ideological factions within each level of government. However, the state officials interviewed for this project did not view efforts to export to the same markets as generating conflict. Instead, all of the states included in this study participate in at least one regional organization focused on export opportunities and market development. As one Arkansas official explained the Mid-South Trade Council, "It formed when states realized they were all going on the same trade shows and spending precious state resources for separate registration fees." Other state officials also noted that efforts to work with other states or in regional organizations resulted from specific needs and are often informal. A state trade official characterized Maryland's inter-state relations as:

...cooperative in trade and competitive in investment. The regional offices [operated by the state of Maryland] work with the states located near them and the overseas offices are shared with other states. The office applies for grants with other states. These relationships tend to be informal and are based on states with common interests rather than border states.

Federal aid was one factor helping to establish cooperative inter-state and intergovernmental relationships. For example, there is extensive federal-state cooperation in agricultural research, education, rural development, and trade. Many of the states surveyed in this research work closely with the Foreign Agricultural Service or with regional agricultural trade groups that are largely funded by USDA. Federal aid was also a factor promoting cooperative ventures in environmental protection. Several of the states surveyed for this report also participated in environmental partnerships in East Asia supported by the Council of State Governments/US-AEP's State Environmental Initiative program (see Figure 2.8).

Trade officials in the states tended to be very positive about their relationships with federal counterparts. Virtually all described their relations with federal agencies in positive or very positive terms. Several used terms like "excellent" and "wonderful" (see Figure 2.9). These favorable assessments were confirmed by actions, as well. In about one half of the states surveyed, state and federal trade offices were deliberately housed in the same building. In several cases, staff and resources were shared between federal and state agencies. State officials in Oklahoma and Missouri are housed in federal office facilities, for example. By the same token, the state trade offices in New Mexico and Texas housed employees of the U.S. Department of Commerce; and both parties shared support staff, utilities, and materials. "I feel like I'm part of them," said the director of New Mexico's District Export Council, a federal official, describing her relations with state trade officials. "It truly is a partnership. We have basically merged."

Even where trade officials are housed separately, most attempt to share information, trade leads, and referrals with each other. The result can be strong ties and closely linked services. "Our relations with federal staff are almost incestuous," said one west coast state director. Similarly, in Maryland, a federal Commerce official maintained that his staff "knows more about the state programs than we do about our own federal programs. Every two weeks there is a transaction meeting of [federal, state, and local] trade specialists in the state international business office." A Maryland state official painted a similar portrait:

> We don't spend time distinguishing ourselves from the Department of Commerce. We work together and know what services each offers and try to help companies through the most appropriate office. There is a free interchange of ideas between the staffs.

In fact, none of the state officials reported conflictual relationships with either their federal or state counterparts. Instead, the overwhelming response to the challenges of the global economy focused on shared strategies for maximizing limited resources.

Figure 2.8: Indicators of Cooperative Inter-State and Intergovernmental Relationships

State	Self-assessment of state/fed relations	Recipient of MDCP Grant	Member of regional trade/agricultural trade organization	Co-located state/fed offices	Recipient os US-AEP Grant
Alabama	Helpful				ARC, MSTC, SGPB, SUSTA
Alaska	Good	X		X	PNWER, WUSATA
Arkansas	Good				MSTC, SGPB, SUSTA
California	Good	X	X	X	WUSATA
Colorado	Very Good	X	X		WUSATA
Florida	Supportive	X		X	SGPB, SUSTA
Hawaii	Very Good		X	X	WUSATA
Illinois	Excellent		X	X	CGLG, MIATCO
Indiana	Helpful				CGLG, MIATCO
Kentucky	Very Good		X		ARC, MSTC, SGPB, SUSTA
Maine	Very Good	X		X	EUSAFEC, NEG/CP, YTI
Maryland	Helpful	X	X	X	ARC, MARTG, SUSTA
Minnesota	Helpful		X	X	CGLG, MIATCO
Missouri	Very Good	X		X	CSTI, MIATCO, SGPB
Montana	Supportive			X	PNWER, WUSATA
Nebraska	Helpful				CSTI, MIATCO
New Mexico	Very Good	X	X	X	WUSATA
New York	Very Good	X	X	X	ARC, CGLG, EUSAFEC, MARTG, YTI
North Carolina	Very Good		X	X	ARC, KUSEC, SGPB, SUSTA, SEUSJC
Oklahoma	Helpful	X	X		SGPB, SUSTA
Oregon	Very Good	X	X	X	PNWER, WUSATA
Tennessee	Very Good		X		ARC, MSTC, SGPB, SUSTA
Texas	Excellent	X	X	X	SUSTA
Virginia	Supportive			X	ARC, MARTG, SGPB, SUSTA
Washington	Very Good	X	X	X	PNWER, WUSATA

Figure 2.9: State Relations with Federal Agencies in International Trade

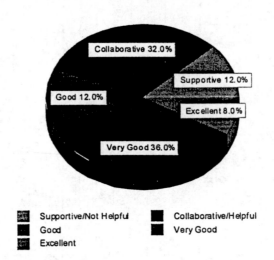

Supportive/Not Helpful   Collaborative/Helpful
Good   Very Good
Excellent

STATE POLICY AND THE DYNAMICS OF GLOBALIZATION

Over the past two decades, states have become increasingly involved in issues of foreign trade and international affairs. During this time, their international activities have grown in scope, scale, and sophistication. Since the late 1970s, state and local governments increased their involvement in international affairs in each of the functional areas examined in this report: trade, agriculture, environmental protection, and education. States have expanded their activities most aggressively in the areas of trade and economic development. Available data on the period between 1984 and 1998 show that state spending on international trade promotion tripled, state trade staffs more than doubled, and the number of overseas trade offices increased from 55 to 152. During this same period, several other important changes occurred as well: 1) the geographic focus of state trade activities broadened, as states directed more attention to countries in Asia and Latin America; 2) educational exchanges and sister city/sister state relationships proliferated; and 3) new forms of public-private partnerships were developed.

Major state and local involvement in international affairs is still relatively new and has not been fully institutionalized. In most states, spending on international activities slowed sharply in the early 1990s and has since remained volatile. Outside of trade, international involvement in fields like environmental protection and international education has been experimental and highly variable. In many states, budgets for international affairs activities have been unstable and subject to wide swings in appropriations levels. Data collected by the National Association of State Development Agencies indicate that the rate of state spending on international activities slowed dramatically in the 1990s under combined pressure from economic recession, state expenditure limitations, and strong competition from other fiscal priorities. After doubling between 1982 and 1986 and doubling again from 1986 to 1990, state spending on international trade activities grew a mere seven percent in nominal dollars between 1990 and 1994. As a result, a plurality of state officials in both the trade and non-trade fields identified budgetary constraints as the most serious factor limiting their international activities. It contributed to staff reductions in many states, limited the range and quality of services, and stimulated a variety of partnerships.

Differences in state population, resources, and priorities give rise to large differences between states in the scope and scale of their international activities. These differences are least pronounced in agriculture, where states have access to higher levels of federal assistance and where regional trade organizations are most effectively organized. States vary widely in size and resources, and their international activities reflect these differences. In 1998, the international trade budgets of the nation's largest states exceeded spending in the smallest states by a factor of ten. These budgetary differences translated into comparable disparities in staffing and trade services. For example, six of the mostly small states had no overseas trade office in 1998. Although the data are less complete, variations in size and resources also affect the scope and sophistication of state international efforts involving education and the environment. Smaller, rural states face fewer disparities in agriculture, where well-established regional organizations and a long history of federal-state cooperation have enabled them to develop more effective strategies for coping with resource limitations.

State and local governments can play a positive role in U.S. foreign affairs. If economic, environmental, and educational issues continue to grow in relative importance as foreign policy concerns, these positive contributions are likely to expand in the years ahead. Although the national government is granted primary responsibility for foreign policy and national defense under the U.S. Constitution, state and local governments can make important and positive contributions on a variety of trade and foreign policy issues. This is most apparent in economic and education policy, where states possess unique powers, resources, and experience *vis-a-vis* the federal government. State and local governments also possess distinctive capabilities in environmental policy, where they have operational responsibility for most pollution control programs. As national security concerns diminish in importance in the post-Cold War era and as trade, education, and environmental issues grow more prominent, these state and local competencies are likely to increase in international significance.

On those trade and foreign policy issues where states and the federal government share similar or complementary goals, officials from both levels of government have developed strong cooperative relationships. Internal coordination among different state agencies is also most likely on these issues. This study found impressive patterns of close and pervasive federal-state and inter-state cooperation on a variety of international issues where both levels of government and multiple states share common or complementary policy goals. Close cooperation was particularly evident on trade promotion and agricultural issues, where federal and state officials commonly shared information, office space, support services, and financial responsibility for program operations. Cooperative support for educational exchange programs and environmental assistance programs was also widespread. Cooperation and effective coordination within states -- both among different state agencies and between state and local governments -- are also most likely in such cases.

The role of the nation state in foreign policy, therefore, is changing. Such entities are losing their previous monopoly over key elements of sovereignty to other public and private entities, including supranational institutions, currency markets, and subnational governments. The importance of this change, especially for federal systems of government, has been underscored by Daniel J. Elazar (1998: ix):

> The transformation of the international system from one in which politically sovereign states under international law were the only legitimate actors to one in which other entities, particularly the constituent states of federal systems, are also involved is one of the major developments of the post-World War II period.

The value of state-level contributions may grow increasingly important. As David Beam (1998: 388) has suggested, the value of a decentralized federal system may be enhanced by the demands of a global economy:

> Under conditions of global competition and rapid technological change, a large nation composed of multiple political and economic centers, each striving to secure its own economic advantage, will be better able to advance the welfare of its citizens than a large nation dominated by a single political and economic center.

This does not imply that there is no role for the federal government to play in trade and economic development issues, however. The federal government's capacity to "speak with one voice" on foreign policy and trade negotiations, its international network of overseas embassies and consulates, and its intelligence and data collection capabilities are indispensable. The federal government's financial resources and capacity to provide support to smaller states and regional trade entities are also invaluable and should be expanded. Finally, the demonstrated capacity for states, localities, and the federal government to share resources and to work cooperatively on international economic development issues, which this research has clearly documented, suggests the value in continuing and expanding these areas of cooperation.

The world's political economy is changing; and the American states are well positioned to adapt to and take advantage of these changes. Many states need to make additional investments in order to be productive actors in the international arena, however. In addition, states should act to stabilize and institutionalize their international activities if they seek to maximize their effectiveness.

REFERENCES

Archer, S.H. and S.M. Maser. 1989. "State Export Promotion for Economic Development." *Economic Development Quarterly* 3: 235-242.

Beam, D.R. 1993. "Reinventing Federalism: State-Local Government Roles in the New Economic Order," in L.J. O'Toole, Jr., Ed., *American Intergovernmental Relations*, 2nd Ed. Washington, D.C.: CQ Press.

Cavusgil, T. and M.R. Czinkota. 1990. *International Perspectives on Trade Promotion and Assistance*. New York: Quorum Books.

Clearinghouse on State International Policies. 1996. May. Chapel Hill, NC: Corporation for Enterprise Development, Newsletter of the State International Policy Network.

Conlan, T.J. and M.A. Sager. 1997. *International Dimensions of American Federalism: State Policy Responses to a Changing Global Environment*. Washington, D.C.: U.S.-Asia Environmental Partnership.

Conway, C. and W.E. Nothdurft. 1996. *The International State: Crafting a Statewide Trade Development System*. Washington, D.C.: The Aspen Institute.

Elazar, D.J. 1988. "Introduction," in I.D. Duchacek, D. Latouche, and G. Stevenson, Eds., *Perforated Sovereignties and International Relations: Trans-Sovereign Contacts of Subnational Governments*. New York: Greenwood.

Fosler, R.S. 1988. "The State Economic Role in Perspective," pp. 8-18 in R.S. Fosler, Ed., *The New Economic Role of American States*. New York: Oxford University Press.

Fry, E.H. 1998. *The Expanding Role of State and Local Governments in U.S. Foreign Affairs*. New York: Council on Foreign Relations Press.

Henkin, L. 1996. *Foreign Affairs and the United States Constitution*, 2d. Ed. New York: Oxford University Press.

Kincaid, J. 1990. "State and Local Governments Go International." *Intergovernmental Perspective* 16: 6-9.

Kline, J.M. 1983. *State Government Influence in U.S. International Economic Policy*. Lexington, MA: Lexington Books.

Latouche, D. 1988. "State Building and Foreign Policy at the Subnational Level," in I. Duchacek, D. Latouche, and G. Stevenson, Eds., *Perforated Sovereignties and International Relations: Trans-sovereign Contacts of Subnational Governments*. New York: Greenwood Press.

Matthews, J. 1997. "Power Shift." *Foreign Affairs* 76: 50-66.

National Association of State Development Agencies. 1994. *State Export Program Database*. National Association of State Development Agencies.

Scheiber, H.N. 1993. "International Economic Policies and the State Role in U.S. Federalism: A Process Revolution?" pp. 65-91 in D.M. Brown and E.H. Fry, Eds., *States and Provinces in the International Economy*, Vol. 2. Berkeley: University of California, Institute of Governmental Studies Press.

Slaughter, A.M. 1997. "The Real New World Order." *Foreign Affairs* 76: 183-197.

Chapter 3

FOREIGN DIRECT INVESTMENT IN THE AMERICAN STATES: POLICY AND MANAGERIAL ISSUES

Kuotsai Tom Liou

Over the past two decades, American state governments have become strongly involved in various activities to promote their economic development. The activities emphasized include, but are not limited to, such strategies as providing financial incentives to reduce business production costs, minimizing government regulation and control over enterprises, and creating new firms, technologies, and markets (Leicht and Jenkins, 1994). The active involvement of states has established a new and entrepreneurial role for state governments in their overall economic development activities (Clark, 1986; Eisinger, 1988; Fosler, 1988a). The new entrepreneurial role of American states in promoting economic development focuses on not only domestic but also international economic activities (Kline, 1983, 1984a & 1984b; Luke and Caiden, 1989; McIntyre, 1983; Neuse, 1982). Major international activities that the states emphasized in their economic development programs consist of increasing exports to other countries, encouraging foreign investment, and encouraging tourists from other countries to visit their states (Liou, 1993).

The issue of incoming direct foreign investment or FDI[1] (as opposed to the outward US investment, which results in unemployment and the "hollowing out" of US industry, or to incoming "portfolio" investment in US stocks and bonds) has become fairly controversial (Liou, 1993). On the positive side, some scholars (Becker, 1989; Glickman and Woodward, 1989; Graham and Krugman, 1989) maintain that FDI contributes to our economy by promoting U.S. employment, technology progress, and international competitiveness. On the negative side, others (Choate, 1990; Tolchin and Tolchin, 1988)

---

[1]Foreign investment in the U.S. is classified as FDI when ownership, directly or indirectly, by a foreign person or business amounts to 10 percent or more of the voting securities of an incorporated U.S. business enterprise, or an equivalent interest in an unincorporated U.S. business enterprise (McGuire, 1993: 1-2).

criticized the increase of FDI and expressed concerns about foreign ownership of American real estate, control over our national resources, influence over our politics, and even a potential threat to our national security.

This chapter examines the development of FDI in the American states during the past two decades. The study first describes the growth of FDI in the United States since the 1970s. It then evaluates research findings concerning major factors determining FDI location. More detailed data on the distribution of FDI in American regions and states are then analyzed. Finally, the study discusses several important public management and policy issues that are related to the development of FDI.

FOREIGN DIRECT INVESTMENT IN THE UNITED STATES

To understand the development of FDI in the American states, we need to examine the general background of FDI in the United States during the past several decades. This section examines two important issues concerning this topic. The first charts the increase of FDI over 1970-1994; and the second summarizes the major reasons that have been used to explain this increase.

The Increase of FDI in the United States, 1970-1994

Foreign direct investment has risen dramatically in the United States since the 1970s. As presented in Table 3.1, the value of FDI in the United States (FDIUS) increased from $13 billion in 1970 to $506 billion in 1995, an increase of about 38 times. The figures are very impressive when comparing them with those of United States direct investment abroad (USDIA). During the same period, the USDIA increased from $75.5 billion to $711.11 billion, an increase of about 9 times.

The increase of FDI is also evidenced in the analysis of ratios between FDIUS and USDIA. Table 3.1 shows that the ratio increased from 17.6 percent in 1970 to 78.7 percent in 1995, an increase of 4.5 fold. Additionally, the data indicate that the increase occurred especially in the 1980s, from 38.6 percent in 1980 to 96.6 percent in 1989, before dropping back to about 80 percent half a decade later. Clearly, it was due to this rapid growth during the 1980s that FDI has become one of the major public policy issues and attracted the attention of policymakers and the American public (U.S. Department of Commerce, 1995).

**Table 3.1: Position of Foreign Direct Investment in the
United States (FDIUS) and United States Direct Investment
Abroad (USDIA), on a Historical-Cost Basis, 1970-1994***

Year	FDIUS	USDIA	FDIUS/USDIA
1970	13,270	75,480	17.6 %
1971	13,914	82,760	16.8
1972	14,868	89,878	16.5
1973	20,556	101,313	20.3
1974	25,144	110,078	22.8
1975	27,662	124,050	22.3
1976	30,770	136,809	22.5
1977	34,595	149,848	23.1
1978	42,471	167,804	25.3
1979	54,462	192,648	28.3
1980	83,046	215,375	38.6
1981	108,714	228,348	47.6
1982	124,677	207,752	60.0
1983	137,061	207,203	66.1
1984	164,583	211,480	77.8
1985	184,615	230,250	80.2
1986	220,414	259,800	84.8
1987	263,394	314,307	83.8
1988	314,754	335,893	93.7
1989	368,924	381,781	96.6
1990	394,911	430,521	91.7
1991	419,108	467,844	89.6
1992	427,566	502,063	85.2
1993	466,666	564,283	82.7
1994	502,410	621,044	80.9
1995**	560,088	711,621	78.7
(95/70)	(42.2)	(9.4)	

* Book value at year end, in millions of dollars. Covers U.S. firms, including real investments in which foreign interest or ownership was 10 percent of more.
** Preliminary
Sources: Bargas. 1997. pp. 15-36; U.S. Department of Commerce. 1977. p. 856; 1981. p. 834; 1986. p. 798;1991. .p. 794; 1993. p. 798; 1994. p. 808; 1997. pp. 793-795.

Reasons for the Increase of FDI in the United States

To explain the increase of FDI in the United States, researchers (Liou, 1993; McGuire, 1993; McGuire and Landefeld, 1991) have identified several factors that are related to both the domestic and the international environments. First, the good domestic investment environment of the U.S. has been considered as one of the major reasons for the increase of FDI. The good investment environment refers to the stability of the political and legal system, the open attitude toward investment, the large size of the U.S. market, and the buying power of American consumers. Macroeconomic condition also contributed to the rapid growth of FDI in the 1980s. These include such interrelated factors as the relatively rapid economic growth in the U.S., the high interest rate, and the depreciation of the U.S. dollar against major currencies (due to the unrestrained trade imbalance). Similarly, several macroeconomic conditions explained the slowed growth of FDI in the 1990s, such as the unification of Germany, the economic problems in Japan, and the increased investment in Southeast Asia.

In addition, the increase of FDI is affected by the global investment strategies of multinational corporations (MNCs). The advances in telecommunications technology in the mid-1980s greatly enhanced the MNCs' ability to control and manage production and distribution around the globe. For these companies, the FDI investment strategy results in such benefits as avoiding protectionism, circumventing barriers to market entry, reducing transportation costs, and improving quality control and services to a market.

Finally, changes in financial policy have enhanced the activities of FDI. These changes occurred at both the international and domestic levels. Internationally, the liberalization of capital markets (e.g., the decontrol of capital flows) facilitated cross-border investment. Domestically, the deregulation policy and the rise of entrepreneurial states enhanced the ability of state and local governments to attract FDI through various promotion activities. These activities include increasing governors' roles in international economic activities (e.g., overseas business trips), opening and expanding overseas offices, offering various economic incentives, (e.g., financial assistance, tax breaks), using enterprise zones, and devising other nonfinancial incentives and services, including site location assistance and state-local training programs (Kline, 1983; Liou, 1993; Poniachek, 1986).

LOCATION RESEARCH ON FOREIGN DIRECT INVESTMENT IN THE U.S.

The expanding role of state economic development and the increase of FDI in the U.S. have generated interest among researchers to study the major factors that affect location decisions by foreign firms. Similar to those studies of domestic firm location (e.g., Wasylenko, 1981), research on FDI location has focused on two major approaches: 1) attitudinal surveys and 2) empirical analysis. For the attitudinal surveys, researchers designed special questionnaires about potential FDI location factors and surveyed top managers of foreign firms to rank the importance of these factors. For the empirical analysis, researchers developed empirical models, collected objective social and economic data, and conducted sophisticated statistical analyses to test the significance of specific location variables. Both approaches have produced important information about FDI location.

Attitudinal Surveys

Since the late 1970s, research using attitudinal surveys has identified some important factors that are related to foreign's firms' location decisions (Ajami and Ricks, 1981; Haitani and Marquis, 1990; Sokoya and Tillery, 1992; Tong, 1979). These studies have surveyed top executives of foreign firms from different countries, among various industries, and in selected or all regions of the U.S. The major findings of these studies have been consistent regarding major FDI location factors. Table 3.2 provides a summary and comparison of the major factors identified by two studies (Ajami and Ricks, 1981; Sokoya and Tillery, 1992) conducted in the early 1980s and 1990s.

Despite the 10-year difference in the research timeframe, Table 3.2 reveals fairly consistent findings about the factors affecting FDI location that are identified and ranked by business managers. First, it is clear that the rank of these factors has been relatively consistent and stable. The difference between the two rankings of the 26 items included in Table 3.2 ranges from 0 (large U.S. market and U.S. managerial and marketing ability) to 21 (need to be closer to consumers); and nearly two-thirds of them (17 or 65%) changed ranks by four or less. Second, eight of the top ten factors identified in 1992 were also ranked in the top ten of the 1981 list. These factors are large U.S. market, search for new markets, need for growth, desire for profit, attractive political climate in the U.S., attractive U.S. attitude toward foreign investment, preserve markets that were established by exporting, and desire to compete abroad by employing technological, managerial, or financial advantages. The two factors that made the top ten list in 1992 but not 1981 are need to be closer to consumers to give better services and the traditional U.S. receptivity to new products, methods, and ideas. The factor of "need to be closer to consumers" is especially important because it has by far the biggest improvement in rank (jumping from 24th to 3rd) and reflects a change of managerial attitudes.

Finally, the two surveys did not provide strong evidence to support the importance or efficacy of public incentive policies. The factor of "to enjoy local incentives" ranked 16th in the 1992 survey and 18th in the 1981 survey. The attitude toward this factor was relatively stable and did not change significantly. The findings here have also been consistent with those of other studies. For example, Tong (1979: 57) reported that the factor of government incentives ranked 27th in a total of 32 location factors; and Haitani and Marquis (1990: 43) found that executives of Japanese-affiliated firms rank government incentive plans secondary to other factors such as market access, available labor, degree of unionization, hospitality, and transportation.

Empirical Analysis

The empirical studies of FDI location adopted quantitative models and variables that had been developed in the studies of domestic firm location decisions. In general, these studies tested empirical models with stepwise regression analysis of aggregate state data (Little, 1978; McConnell, 1980) or conditional logit analysis (emphasized by McFadden, 1974) of individual firms' consideration of general state characteristics (Coughlin, et al.,

1991; Luger and Shetty, 1985). These studies also changed their focus from the general consideration of all industries and sources of countries to the more specialized studies of a particular industry, such as real estate (Gerlowski, et al., 1992), or from a special source country, such as Japan (Woodward, 1992).

Table 3.2: Attitudinal Study of Motive Rankings

Motives	1992	1981	1992-1981
Extremely large U.S. market	1	1	0
Search for new market	2	3	1
Need to be closer to consumers to give better service	3	24	21
General need for growth	4	2	2
General desire for profit	5	7	2
Attractive political climate in the U.S.	6	4	2
Attractive U.S. attitude toward foreign investment	7	6	1
Desire to preserve markets that were established by exporting	8	5	3
Desire to compete abroad by employing technological, managerial, or financial advantages	9	10	1
Traditional U.S. receptivity to new products, methods, and ideas	10	13	3
U.S. managerial and marketing know-how	11	11	0
Attractive U.S. capital markets	12	20	8
Desire for geographic dispersion as a means of spreading risks	13	9	4
Need for assured supplies or resources	14	25	11
Declining value of the U.S. dollar, at the time of investment	15	19	4
To enjoy local incentives (such as taxes, credits, etc.)	16	18	2
Attractive U.S. supplies of important natural resources	17	21	4
Skill and efficiency of U.S. labor force	18	17	1
The possibility of import restrictions on primary products being imported to the U.S.	19	NA	NA
Desire to acquire technologies	20	8	12
Attractive U.S. technology	21	12	9
Desire to integrate forward and backward to reduce dependence on other firms	22	23	1
Desire to hold land or other foreign assets as a hedge against domestic inflation or as a store of value	23	22	1
Investments may be the only way to surmount risks	24	16	8
Comparatively less U.S. government control over business	25	15	10
Fear of further investments in home country because of political unrest	26	14	12

Sources: Ajami and Ricks. 1981. p. 32; Sokoya and Tillery. 1992. p. 73.

Table 3.3: Empirical Analysis of Location Factors

Category	Sample Variable
General Economic Condition	
Regional market demand	Per capita personal income
Industrial agglomeration	Manufacturing establishments per capita
	Annual production manhours in a particular industry
Urban Attraction and Labor Market	
Urban attraction	Urban population as a percentage of total population
Labor market condition	Unemployment rate
	Percentage of unionized employees
	Right to work law
State Public Policy	
Public infrastructure	Highway miles
	Port facilities
	Number of public airport
Tax policy	State corporate income tax structure
	State with a worldwide unitary tax
Promotion incentives	State with tax incentives
	State with financial assistance
	State with employment assistance
	Number of industrial development incentives
General State Characteristics	
Other cost differentials	Energy cost
Climate index	Average annual temperature
Social amenities	Index of social well-being
Land availability	State land excluding federal land
Regional effect	Pacific region (for Japanese investment)

Four major areas have been emphasized in these empirical studies of FDI location: 1) economic conditions, 2) urban attraction and labor markets, 3) state public policy, and 4) general state characteristics. As summarized in Table 3.3, each area consists of a number of factors which, in turn, are measured by several variables. First, regarding the area of economic conditions, researchers believe that regional market demand and industrial agglomeration have a positive impact on location decisions of foreign firms. Second, it was assumed that urban population tends to have a positive effect on FDI, while some labor conditions (e.g., union activities) tend to have a negative impact. The third area comes from the assumption that foreign firms will take advantage of certain public policies (e.g., promotion incentives) and avoid the impact of other policies (e.g., tax policy and structure). Finally, foreign firms may also consider other state characteristics (e.g., climate, land availability) in their location decisions.

Despite the various models and factors emphasized, empirical studies of FDI location decisions have provided some mixed and inconsistent results. For example, some studies found a positive relationship between FDI location and state economic conditions (Coughlin, et al., 1990 & 1991; Woodward, 1992), while others reported no relationship between the two (Little, 1978; McConnell, 1980). Similarly, state unemployment rate has been found to be positively related to FDI location in some studies (Coughlin, et al., 1990 & 1991), negatively related to it in others (Gerlowski, et al., 1992), and not related to FDI at all in still others (Little, 1978; Moore, et al., 1987). In the area of general state characteristics, studies supported the importance of state land availability and FDI (Coughlin, et al., 1990 & 1991; Woodward, 1992), but not of climate (McConnell, 1980; Woodward, 1992).

With regard to state public policies, empirical studies also produced some mixed findings. On the positive side, several studies supported the positive relationship between state transportation and FDI (Coughlin, et al., 1991; Gerlowski, et al., 1992; Glickman and Woodward, 1988). With regard to tax policy and structure, some studies found no relationship between FDI and state corporate income taxes (Moore, et al., 1987; Woodward, 1992), while others showed a negative relationship between FDI and state worldwide unitary tax structure (Coughlin, et al., 1990; Moore, et al., 1987; Woodward, 1992). In particular, these studies did not find any evidence supporting a significant impact of state incentive policies on FDI (Coughlin, et al., 1990; Little, 1978; Luger and Shetty, 1985; McConnell, 1980; Woodward, 1992).

FOREIGN DIRECT INVESTMENT IN AMERICAN REGIONS AND STATES

Recognizing the importance of the findings from the FDI location research, this study is interested in examining the distribution and growth of FDI in the American regions and states over the past two decades. This section provides analyses of the distribution of FDI in 9 regions[2] and 50 states in the years of 1974, 1981, and 1991. These years were selected because of the considerations of data availability and comparison. The analysis focuses on examining gross book value and employment data because they provide information about the impact of FDI on financial and human resources and are the most common measurements in the study of FDI growth.

---

[2]The nine regions are: New England (Maine, New Hampshire, Vermont, Massachusetts, Rhode Island, Connecticut), Middle Atlantic (New York, New Jersey, Pennsylvania), East North Central (Ohio, Indiana, Illinois, Michigan, Wisconsin), West North Central (Minnesota, Iowa, Missouri, North Dakota, South Dakota, Nebraska, Kansas), South Atlantic (Delaware, Maryland, District of Columbia, Virginia, West Virginia, North Carolina, South Carolina, Georgia, Florida), East South Central (Kentucky, Tennessee, Alabama, Mississippi), West South Central (Arkansas, Louisiana, Oklahoma, Texas), Mountain (Montana, Idaho, Wyoming, Colorado, New Mexico, Arizona, Utah, Nevada), and Pacific (Washington, Oregon, California, Alaska, Hawaii).

FDI in Regions

Focusing on regional data, Table 3.4 provides a summary of the distribution of FDI gross book value and employment in 1974, 1981, and 1991. First, the percentage distributions of the book values reveal that, between 1974 and 1991, there was an increase of the percentages in the Pacific, Mountain, and South Atlantic regions, a decrease of the percentages in the Middle Atlantic, East North Central, and West North Central regions, and the same percentages in the New England and East South Central regions. The ranking data indicate improved ranks in the Pacific, Mountain, and South Atlantic regions, the same ranks in the New England, Middle Atlantic, East North Central, and East South Central regions, and decreased ranks in the West North Central and West South Central regions. Finally, the ratio data between 1974 and 1991 show that the Mountain, Pacific, and East South Central regions are the top the three regions in the growth of FDI book values.

Next, the distribution of FDI employment data show increased percentages in six regions (West North Central, South Atlantic, East South Central, West South Central, Mountain, and Pacific), decreased percentages in two regions (Middle Atlantic and East North Central), and the same percentage in one region (New England). The ranking data show an improved rank in South Atlantic, a lower rank in Middle Atlantic, and same ranks in the other regions. The ratio data indicate that the Mountain, West North Central, and South Atlantic regions are the top three regions in the growth of FDI employment.

FDI in States

Similarly, the distributions of FDI book value and employment in all 50 states in 1974, 1981, and 1991 were also analyzed. The top ten states for both book value and employment in 1974 and 1991 are summarized in Table 3.5. Table 3.5 demonstrates, first, the importance and dominance of the top ten states in FDI because these states possessed over 50 percent in both book value and employment in the two years. Second, the ranks of the top ten states in FDI are fairly stable, as other studies have also found (Arpan and Ricks, 1986; Liou, 1993). For example, six states (California, New York, Texas, Illinois, New Jersey, and Ohio) ranked in the top ten on both book value and employment in 1974 and 1991. In addition to these six states, Alaska and Louisiana ranked in the top ten on book value for both years, while Pennsylvania and North Carolina ranked in the top ten on employment in both 1974 and 1991. Florida and Georgia made the top ten for the first time on both lists in 1991 when they replaced Michigan and South Carolina in book value and Michigan and Wisconsin in employment. Considering the FDI distributions in both regions and states, it is important to notice that several states may be located in the least dynamic regions but have but have experienced a strong surge in their own incoming FDI. For example, South Dakota ranked second in the U.S. on FDI growth for both book value and growth, although it is located in the stagnant West North Central region, indicating that its performance must be considered especially strong.

Table 3.4: Gross Book Value (In Millions Of Dollars) And Employment (In Thousands) Of U.S. Affiliates Of Foreign Companies By Regions, 1974, 1981, And 1991

Book Value	1974		1981		1991		Ratio	
	Value (%)	Rank	Value (%)	Rank	Value (%)	Rank	91/74	Rank
Total*	45,454 (100)		187,956 (100)		634,688 (100)		14.0	
New England	1,701 (4)	9	5,686 (3)	9	22,362 (4)	9	13.1	5
M. Atlantic	6,275 (14)	5	20,216 (11)	4	81,353 (13)	5	13.0	6
E. N. Central	6,448 (14)	4	19,215 (10)	5	81,499 (13)	4	12.6	7
W. N. Central	2,622 (6)	6	8,400 (4)	8	30,411 (5)	8	11.6	9
S. Atlantic	6,552 (14)	3	33,271 (18)	3	103,640 (16)	2	15.8	4
E. S. Central	2,138 (5)	7	9,802 (5)	7	34,708 (5)	7	16.2	3
W. S. Central	7,380 (16)	1	34,651 (18)	1	87,919 (14)	3	11.9	8
Mountain	1,805 (4)	8	12,353 (7)	6	36,146 (6)	6	20.0	1
Pacific	6,991 (15)	2	34,409 (18)	2	129,554 (20)	1	18.5	2
Employment	Number (%)	Rank	Number (%)	Rank	Number (%)	Rank	91/74	Rank
Total*	1083.4 (100)		2416.6 (100)		4809.2 (100)		4.4	
New England	61.5 (6)	6	143.9 (6)	6	284.5 (6)	6	4.6	7
M. Atlantic	282.4 (26)	1	480.2 (20)	1	809.0 (17)	3	2.9	9
E. N. Central	206.7 (19)	2	388.6 (16)	3	813.7 (17)	2	3.9	8
W. N. Central	43.1 (4)	8	112.2 (5)	8	262.0 (5)	8	6.1	2
S. Atlantic	166.1 (15)	3	476.0 (20)	2	938.3 (20)	1	5.6	3
E. S. Central	51.6 (5)	7	121.7 (5)	7	275.0 (6)	7	5.3	5
W. S. Central	86.3 (8)	5	268.5 (11)	5	444.7 (9)	5	5.2	6
Mountain	27.7 (3)	9	97.9 (4)	9	203.8 (4)	9	7.4	1
Pacific	139.1 (13)	4	313.3 (13)	4	747.2 (16)	4	5.4	4

*including FDI in other regions (Puerto Rico, Other territories and offshore, foreign)

Sources: *Survey of Current Business*. 1976. p. 48; U.S. Department of Commerce. 1994. p. 809.

Table 3.5: Ranking of Top Ten States in FDI Position and Improvement, 1974 and 1991

Rank	FDI Position				FDI Growth	
	Book Value*		Employment**		Book Value	Employment
	1974	1991	1974	1991	91/74	91/74
Total	$45,454	$634,688	1083.4	4809.2	14.0%	4.4%
1	TX (9%)	CA (13%)	NY (14%)	CA (12%)	NV (145.6%)	NV (17.6%)
2	CA (9%)	TX (10%)	CA (10%)	NY (8%)	SD (34.9%)	SD (16.3%)
3	NY (6%)	NY (7%)	NJ (8%)	TX (6%)	OR (32.8%)	DE (9.9%)
4	LA (6%)	IL (4%)	IL (7%)	IL (5%)	GA (29.1%)	AZ (8.9%)
5	NJ (5%)	OH (4%)	PA (5%)	NJ (5%)	ID (28.6%)	UT (8.7%)
6	IL (4%)	FL (3%)	TX (5%)	OH (5%)	AZ (26.5%)	OR (8.4%)
7	OH (4%)	NJ (3%)	OH (4%)	PA (5%)	KY (24.6%)	FL (8.4%)
8	AK (3%)	AK (3%)	NC (4%)	FL (4%)	FL (22.9%)	MT (8.3%)
9	MI (3%)	LA (3%)	MI (3%)	NC (4%)	IN (21.4%)	NM (8.2%)
10	SC (3%)	GA (3%)	WI (3%)	GA (3%)	CA (20.7%)	NE (7.6%)
Total	(52%)	(53%)	(63%)	(57%)		

*Book value: in millions of dollars

**Employment: in thousands

Sources: *Survey of Current Business*. 1976. p. 48; U.S. Department of Commerce. 1994. p. 809.

Finally, FDI growth rates between 1974 and 1991 were also calculated. Five states (Nevada, South Dakota, Oregon, Arizona, and Florida) made the top ten in the growth of both book value and employment. In addition, Georgia, Idaho, Kentucky, Indiana, and California were in the top ten on book value growth, while Delaware, Utah, Montana, New Mexico, and Nebraska made the top ten for employment growth. These results suggest several broader conclusions. First, FDI has clearly risen significantly in all 50 states between 1974 and 1991 with the largest increase in Nevada (145 percent in gross book value and 17 percent in employment) and the smallest in Vermont (7 percent in gross book value and 2 percent in employment). Second these growth data are important because they reveal the importance of FDI for some small states that is not apparent from the absolute figures. For example, Nevada and South Dakota ranked first and second in FDI growth despite very low rankings in terms of their absolute scores. Thus, such states have evidently been making special efforts to attract foreign investment.

PUBLIC POLICY AND MANAGEMENT ISSUES

This study has examined the development of FDI in the American states during the past two decades. These data on the growth of foreign direct investment suggest two broader issues about FDI that will almost certainly increase in importance as the new century opens. The first concerns whether or not state incentive policies for attracting FDI are effective; and the second involves changes in public management practices that increased foreign contacts are bringing to state and local government.

State Incentive Policy

One of the major controversial policy issues associated with FDI is the utilization of promotion incentives by state and local governments. These financial incentives may be either direct or indirect (Liou, 1993; Luger and Shetty, 1985; Poniachek, 1986). Direct financial incentives consist of various types of assistance and tax breaks. The former refers to industrial development bonds and mortgages, loan guarantee programs, direct loan programs, and development credit corporations; while the latter refers to tax reductions and exemptions, as well as to tax credits and preferential assessment. Indirect financial incentives include such services as site location assistance, rail and highway connections, roads, water and sewage facilities, state and local training programs, and assistance in conducting market studies.

Despite various types of services, the effectiveness of state incentive policy has not been documented by any FDI location research. As revealed in the summary of location research, both attitudinal and empirical studies of FDI location did not provide strong evidence to support the effectiveness of the incentive policy. In the attitudinal studies, the provision of state incentive services was not considered by managers of foreign firms as one of the top factors affecting location decisions. The empirical studies of FDI location did not find any significant relationships between FDI location and state incentive services. The finding of consistent and stable distributions of FDI among major states reported in this study and other research further questions the effectiveness of incentives.

In addition to the issue of effectiveness, the impact of state FDI incentive policy has not been seriously evaluated based on the criteria of efficiency and equity. The evaluation of the efficiency of state FDI incentive policy requires comparison studies of the benefits and costs of various incentive programs, but only a few case studies of incentive costs have been conducted (Glickman and Woodward, 1989). Thus, future research on FDI needs to develop cost-benefit models and to examine the impact of state FDI incentives, similarly to existing analyses of domestic industries. The evaluation of the equity of state FDI incentive policies calls for studies to examine whether the location of foreign firms, influenced by state incentive services, provides equal employment opportunities for minorities. The equity issue of FDI location is important because some studies of domestic industrial development find a negative association between communities with more black population and plant locations (Markusen, et al., 1987; Reginald, 1983). With regard to FDI, Cole and Deskins (1988) observed similar negative findings in site location and employment patterns by Japanese auto firms in America.

Public Management Issues

The rise of FDI in the American states during the past two decades has raised several important managerial issues for state public administrators. One of the issues is for state officials to promote a general positive investment climate in their states. Understanding the limitation and shortcomings of incentive policies, public administrators, especially economic development officials, should work hard to evaluate their overall investment programs and to provide such desirable features as a capable and motivated workforce, a sound physical infrastructure, well-managed natural resources, an attractive quality of life, and fiscal soundness (Fosler, 1988b).

In addition to the improvement of investment programs, public administrators also need to refine their managerial skills in such areas as strategic thinking, catalytic leadership, and multicultural learning (Luke and Caiden, 1989: 90-91). In other words, public administrators need to think globally (i.e., seeking opportunities internationally) and act locally (i.e. developing longer-term goals and plans to integrate local resources and international interests). It is also important for public administrators to improve their interpersonal skills in order to build coalitions among key public and private stakeholders around important global-local issues. Especially, there is an increasing need for public administrators to understand the cultures, markets, languages, and government structures of other countries

The issue of multicultural understanding and learning is especially important in the case of Japanese-affiliated FDI because of the lack of understanding between the American public and Japanese firms. For example, a public opinion survey showed that more Americans (64 percent of the respondents) believe that Japanese investments in the U.S. pose a threat to U.S. economic independence than European investments (37 percent), even though Europeans invest more in the U.S. than do the Japanese (Miko and

Weilant, 1991: 15). In the study of perceptions of FDI among business and professional people in Montana, Karahan and his associates (1995) noticed that positive perceptions about FDI dropped about 8 percentage points for Japanese FDI (i.e., from 65 percent for all FDI to 57 percent for Japanese FDI). It is interesting to note that government officials had a larger percentage drop (16 percentage points, from 73 percent to 57 percent) in positive views toward Japanese FDI than did business people (7 percentage points, from 61 percent to 54 percent) and chamber of commerce and economic development organization members (8 percentage points, from 88 percent to 80 percent). On the other hand, other studies (Cole and Deskins, 1988) also found that Japanese firms and managers do not understand American culture and society and that such misunderstandings are reflected in their decisions about site location and hiring practices, especially with regard to African American communities.

To improve multicultural understanding, we need to provide some kind of cross-cultural training to public officials. The selection of appropriate training methods should be based on such criteria as the degree of cultural distance, the degree of job novelty, and the degree of interaction (Chadwin, et al., 1995: 520). The training methods considered range from factual approaches (e.g., area briefings, lectures, books) to analytical ones (e.g., films, classroom language training, case studies, sensitivity training) to experimental programs (e.g., interactive language training, role playing, simulations, field trips, in-country training).

CONCLUSION

In sum, the considerable increase of FDI since the late 1970s has brought changes and challenges to public management and policy across the American states. Based on the findings of location research and state FDI distributions, the present study has addressed such issues as the growth of FDI in small states, the effectiveness, efficiency, and equity of state incentive policies, the importance of the general investment environment, and the need for multicultural understanding and training. To further understand the impact of FDI, future research should explore other policy and management issues such as the comprehensive evaluation of state programs for international business development, the impact of FDI on national security, and intergovernmental cooperation in international economic policies. The understanding of these issues will enhance the role of government agencies and public administrators in this age of global competitiveness (Tolchin, 1996).

REFERENCES

Ajami, R.A. and D.A. Ricks. 1981. "Motives of Non-American Firms Investing in the United States." *Journal of International Business Studies* 12: 25-34.

Arpan, J.S. and D.A. Ricks. 1986. "Foreign Direct Investment in the U.S., 1974-1984." *Journal of International Business Studies* 17: 149-153.

Bargas, S.E. 1997. "The Foreign Direct Investment Position in the United States on a Historical-Cost Basis: Country and Industry Detail for 1995 and Changes in Geographic Composition Since 1982," pp. 15-36 in U.S. Department of Commerce, *Foreign Direct Investment in the United States: An Update*. Washington, D.C.: U.S. Government Printing Office.

Becker, M. 1989. *Myths about Foreign Investment*. Washington, D.C.: Citizens for a Sound Economy Foundation.

Chadwin, M.L., S.E. Rogers, and P.S. Kim. 1995. "Dealing with *Them*: Preparing State and Local Officials for the Cross-Cultural Challenge." *Public Administration Review* 55: 517-521.

Choate, P. 1990. *Agents of Influence: How Japan's Lobbyists in the United States Manipulate America's Political and Economic System*. New York: Alfred Knopf.

Clark, M. 1986. *Revitalizing State Economies*. Washington, D.C.: National Governors' Association.

Cole, R.E. and R.R. Deskins, Jr. 1988. "Racial Factors in Site Location and Employment Patterns of Japanese Auto Firms in America." *California Management Review* 31: 9-22.

Coughlin, C.C., J.V. Terza, and V. Arromdee. 1990. "State Government Effects on the Location of Foreign Direct Investment." *Regional Science Perspectives* 20: 194-207.

Coughlin, C.C., J.V. Terza, and V. Arromdee. 1991. "State Characteristics and the Location of Foreign Direct Investment within the United States." *The Review of Economics and Statistics* 73: 675-683.

Eisinger, P. 1988. *The Rise of the Entrepreneurial State*. Madison: University of Wisconsin Press.

Fosler, R.S. 1988a. *The New Economic Role of the American States*. New York: Oxford University Press.

Fosler, R.S. 1988b. "State Economic Development Strategies." *Economic Development Review* 6: 45-49.

Gerlowski, D.A., H.G. Fung, and F. Shahrokh. 1992. "An Initial Assessment of the Location Preferences of Foreign Investors in U.S. Real Estate: 1980-1988." *Southern Business & Economic Journal* 15: 129-146.

Glickman, N.J. and D.P. Woodward. 1988. "The Location of Foreign Direct Investment in the United States: Patterns and Determinants." *International Regional Science Review* 11: 137-154.

Glickman, N.J. and D.P. Woodward. 1989. *The New Competitors: How Foreign Investors Are Changing the U.S. Economy*. New York: Basic Books.

Graham, E.M. and P.R. Krugman. 1989. *Foreign Direct Investment in the United States*. Washington, D.C.: Institute for International Economics.

Haitani, K. and C.T. Marquis. 1990. "Japanese Investment in the Southeast United States: Factors, Obstacles, and Opportunities." *Economic Development Review* 8: 42-48.

Karahan, R., L. Sitki, B. James, and S. Akis. 1995. "Attitudes toward Foreign Direct Investment in the Rural United States: The Case of Montana." *International Journal of Management* 12: 78-82.

Kline, J.M. 1983. *State Government Influence in U.S. International Economic Policy.* Lexington, MA: D.C. Health.

Kline, J.M. 1984a. "The International Economic Interests of U.S. States." *Publius* 14(4): 81-94.

Kline, J.M. 1984b. "The Expanding International Agenda for State Governments." *State Government* 57(1): 2-6.

Leicht, K.T. and J.C. Jenkins. 1994. "Three Strategies of State Economic Development: Entrepreneurial, Industrial Recruitment, and Deregulation Policies in the American States." *Economic Development Quarterly* 8: 256-269.

Liou, K.T. 1993. "Foreign Direct Investment in the United States: Trends, Motives, and the State Experience." *American Review of Public Administration* 23: 1-17.

Little, J.S. 1978. "Locational Decisions of Foreign Direct Investors in the United States." *New England Economic Review* 10(4): 43-63.

Luger, M.I. and S. Shetty. 1985. "Determinants of Foreign Plant Start-ups in the United States: Lessons for Policymakers in the Southeast." *Vanderbilt Journal of Transnational Law* 18: 223-245.

Luke, J.S. and G.E. Caiden. 1989. "Coping with Global Interdependence," pp. 83-93 in J.L. Perry, Ed., *Handbook of Public Administration.* San Francisco: Jossey-Bass Publishers.

Markusen, A., P. Hall, and A. Glasmeier. 1987. *High Tech America.* Boston: Allen and Unwin.

McConnell, J.E. 1980. "Foreign Direct Investment in the United States." *Annals of the Association of American Geographers* 70: 259-270.

McFadden, D. 1974. "Conditional Logit Analysis of Qualitative Choice Behavior," pp. 105-142 in P. Zarembka, Ed., *Frontiers in Econometrics.* New York: Academic Press.

McGuire, S.O. 1993. "Introduction and Key Findings," pp. 1-6 in *Foreign Direct Investment in the United States: An Update.* Washington, D.C.: U.S. Department of Commerce.

McGuire, S.O. and J.S. Landefeld. 1991. "Factors Driving Foreign Direct Investment," pp. 9-12 in U.S. Department of Commerce, *Foreign Direct Investment in the United States: Review and Analysis of Current Developments.* Washington, D.C.: U.S. Government Printing Office.

McIntyre, J.R. 1983. "The Role of State Governments as International Economic Actors." *Southern Review of Public Administration* 7: 465-488.

Miko, C.J. and E. Weilant. Eds. 1991. *Opinions '90.* New York: Gale Research Inc.

Moore, M.L., B.M. Steece, and C.W. Swenson. 1987. "An Analysis of the Impact of State Income Tax Rates and Bases on Foreign Investment." *The Accounting Review* 42: 671-685.

Neuse, S.M. 1982. "State Activities in International Trade." *State Government* 55 (2): 57-64.

Poniachek, H.A. 1986. *Direct Foreign Investment in the United States.* Lexington, MA: D.C. Heath.

Reginald, S. 1983. "Business Said to Have Barred New Plants in Largely Black Communities." *New York Times*, February 15.

Sokoya, S.K. and K.R. Tillery. 1992. "Motives of Foreign MNCs Investing in the United States and Effect of Company Characteristics." *The International Executive* 34: 65-80.

Survey of Current Business. 1976. 56: May.

Tolchin, M. and S. Tolchin. 1988. *Buying into America: How Foreign Money Is Changing the Face of Our Nation*. New York: Times Books.

Tolchin, S.J. 1996. "The Globalist from Nowhere: Making Governance Competitive in the International Environment." *Public Administration Review* 56: 1-8.

Tong, H.M. 1979. *Plant Location Decisions of Foreign Manufacturing Investors*. Ann Arbor, MI: UMI Research Press.

U.S. Department of Commerce. 1976. *Survey of Current Business, May*. Washington, D.C.: U.S. Government Printing Office.

U.S. Department of Commerce. 1977, 1981, 1986, 1991, 1993, 1994 & 1997. *Statistical Abstract of the United States*. Washington, D.C.: U.S. Government Printing Office.

U.S. Department of Commerce. 1995. *Foreign Direct Investment in the United States: An Update*. Washington, D.C.: U.S. Department of Commerce.

Wasylenko, M. 1981. "The Location of Firms: The Role of Taxes and Fiscal Incentives," pp. 150-190 in R. Bahl, Ed., *Urban Government Finance: Emerging Trends*. Beverly Hills, CA: Sage.

Woodward, D.P. 1992. "Locational Determinants of Japanese Manufacturing Start-ups in the United States." *Southern Economic Journal* 58: 690-708.

Chapter 4

GLOBALIZATION'S IMPACT ON STATE AND LOCAL POLICY: THE RISE OF REGIONAL CLUSTER-BASED ECONOMIC DEVELOPMENT STRATEGIES[1]

Claire L. Felbinger and James E. Robey

The business of business, the business of politics, and, therefore, the business of economic development is global. This fact is not going to change. Mander (1996) has argued that globalization involves the most fundamental redesign of political and economic arrangements since the Industrial Revolution. There is certainly evidence that globalization has had a deleterious impact on identifiable classes of citizens. Examples of these impacts include residential segregation (Bashi and Hughes, 1997), urban housing (Bartelt, 1997), and education (Dimitriadis and Kamberelis, 1997). Haynes and Stough (1997) suggest there is an insufficiently articulated federal policy to respond to these and other effects of globalization. Rather than focus on these negative effects and on "combating" these effects, however, the argument here is that restructuring will continue and that this includes restructuring current notions of the roles of state and local governments in the process.

It seems reasonable to conclude that in order to be successful in a global economy, state and local policy must also be redesigned to operate in this environment. The purpose of this chapter is to propose proactive policies which allow state and local governments to participate in the global economy, offering the opportunities and venues for effective development. The first section develops the argument that the changing economic conditions associated with globalization call for a new approach to state-local economic development policy. It outlines three assumptions which, the authors think, are critical to drive successful state and local economic development policy in a global environment and then examine the theoretical underpinnings of these assumptions. The

---

[1]Thanks to Claudette L. Sevin at Nicholls State University for editing and other assistance.

major part of the analysis then describes this new strategy of "regional cluster-based economic development," drawing extensively upon a case study of Cleveland's economic revitalization.

ASSUMPTIONS OF THE NEW APPROACH

The first assumption is, perhaps, the most difficult for state and local officials to operationalize (although some can deal with it conceptually): for economic development, cities and states are no longer meaningful units of analysis. According to Wilson (1997: 11), "Spatial barriers [have] become artifacts of the past, simple administrative units that enclose globally tinged inhabitants." While we would not go so far as to say they are not relevant in any way, there are three aspects of this situation that governmental officials need to understand. Most fundamentally, globalization has broken the linkage between business entities and place-based employees. Cities can be discarded by business enterprises when conditions are not favorable. Even when cities offer as much as they legally can in terms of tax abatements, infrastructure investments, or other amenities, businesses are free to relocate within the region, to another region, or to another country. Consequently, no single state or local governmental unit can possibly deal with global economic issues unilaterally. Global economic development strategies cannot be based on a simple smoke-stack chasing strategy. Instead, regional strategies are more appropriate than any focusing exclusively on central cities, suburbs or even states. Moreover, a single definition of what constitutes a "region" does not exist. In most cases, "state" as a region is too big; and "city" as a region is too small. In Cleveland, an argument will be made that its economic development region is multi-county. In New York it almost assuredly is multi-state. We will report later on one regional strategy developed in greater Cleveland -- cluster-based economic development.

The second assumption is that regions cannot depend on developing only *specific* capacities, but rather *general* capacities which ensure a flexible workforce. In particular, since we do not know which specific capacities will be required in the future, the best strategy is to prepare individuals who can transfer and translate skills into diverse industries as the need emerges. That is, human capital development must assume a central role in economic development strategies (Clarke and Gaile, 1998). Institutions currently providing training programs, hence, should not keep training people in non-needed skills, even if they are providing excellent training. Although this seems logical, we know of one technical college in the Midwest which trained highly skilled welders to supply the welding and fabrication needs of heavy industry -- and kept providing this excellent training after those manufacturing plants closed or relocated. Although globalization has de-linked business from place, people may not be so easily de-linked from their personal "place" for a variety of reasons.

The third assumption is that any effective economic development policy in a global environment must rely on partnerships among state and local governments, public and private firms, non-profit organizations, universities, and foundations. In the global environment the roles which each of these participants might play will be restructured as well. The policies proposed in this chapter reflect these underlying assumptions.

THE THEORETICAL BASE: SCHUMPETER'S CONCEPT OF ECONOMIC DEVELOPMENT

Joseph Schumpeter (1983) suggests that aspects of the economy exist in one of two states: one he calls the "circular flow" and one he calls "discontinuous change." The circular flow of economies is based on a maintenance of a *status quo*. Changes in the local economy occur in increased employment and wealth generated by providing more of the same goods and services. Schumpeter labeled this type of activity as "economic growth," doing more of the same. For example, if the local economy is agriculturally based, increased agriculture production results in economic growth. Likewise, if the local economy is based in primary metals, increased metal production creates economic growth. Schumpeter (1983: 61) concludes that the "economic life [of a community] from a stand point of a 'circular flow,' is running on in channels essentially the same year after year." This economic growth or circular flow is consistent with the adaptation required for a global economic strategy.

This does not mean that an economy cannot change. Schumpeter (1983: 63) expects the local economy to grow, but the circular flow economy "calls forth no qualitatively new phenomena, but only processes adaptation of the same kind of changes in the natural data." Schumpeter indicated that innovation, adaptation and evolution can occur within these economies. However, this change occurs within existing industries and their structures. A good example of this type of change is the evolution from standard typewriters, to electronic versions, to the IBM Selectric, and then to machines with increasing capabilities such as memory and spell check, and finally to dedicated word processors with video screens. For Schumpeter, this is "growth" -- doing and producing more of the same thing. However, while potentially increasing the pool of wealth within the community, this does not raise the standard of living. The evolution of the typewriter allowed the same firms, through adaptation, innovation and modification to continue to produce an increasingly sophisticated but essentially undifferentiated product.

Schumpeter (1983: 65) suggested that real increases in the standard of living come through "economic development." This occurs through the use of new "combinations" of resources that produce new products. These new combinations are changes in the production functions in which products previously produced are replaced with new types of goods (and assumedly services). It is the development of new products or "innovations" on the part of the producer that "initiates economic change, and consumers are educated by him and if necessary; they are taught to want new things." This stimulation of new needs driven by new products accelerates local economic growth. This is the same type of stimulus which is necessary in a globalized economy. An argument can be made that changes in demands for products, along with the changing of actors responding to these demands, can push a local area out of a global strategy, if a region cannot respond to the new economic requisites. Thus, globalization goes one step beyond what Schumpeter calls economic change -- it is the economic development of regional economies responding to these changes.

These changes are "spontaneous and discontinuous" and cause a "disturbance of equilibrium, which forever alters and displaces the equilibrium state previously existing" (Schumpeter, 1983: 64). Essentially, innovations occur which are unexpected or unforeseen and which compete for resources with existing types of production, particularly for capital, labor and space. Schumpeter makes it clear that prior to the innovation, one cannot anticipate the recombining of resources needed for the innovation. The "resources" that are required for these "re-combinations" may be labor, capital and raw material inputs. However, if the new products are able to compete successfully for these resources, they must produce a product that in the aggregate has more value or return on investment than the returns from the previous uses. Because of this lack of prior knowledge, one cannot anticipate what the labor, material or capital needs will be in advance of developing the good or product.

To continue the typewriter metaphor, the computer with its central processing unit (CPU) has replaced the typewriter as a means of creating business and personal communications. The firms currently dominating the computer industry are generally different from those that dominated the typewriter industry; and the inputs into building computers are different, as are the skill sets of labor. While some artifacts (such as the distinctive QWERTY keyboard) were carried from the typewriter to the computer, very little else has been adaptable. Computerization was a radical departure from the typewriter. Thus, the needs of the industry that grew around the computer could not have been anticipated prior to its invention.

A dilemma for local economies is created because of Schumpeter's concept of change. Increases in the standard of living result from discontinuous change. But, if prior to change or innovation, the needs surrounding production cannot be known, then how does a local economy prepare for these shifts to occur? The answer to this dilemma comes, at least in part, from a regional economic view. In this view, subregional entities do to not attempt to compete with each other for new firms and employment, but act in concert to provide an attractive and profitable location in which firms will find the location desirable and profitable. Thus, local and state governments can benefit, both directly and indirectly, from expansion housed with and around their jurisdictions. It is clear that labor and capital are both mobile and move freely across political boundaries and that benefits extend from new and retained investment beyond the jurisdictions in which they reside. Regional economies, hence, are the ones best equipped to respond to global demands

IMPLICATIONS FOR STATE-LOCAL DEVELOPMENT STRATEGIES: REGIONAL CLUSTER-BASED DEVELOPMENT

Traditionally, much of the economic development activity at both the state and local level has taken the form of either smoke-stack chasing or addressing some type of "market failure." Both issues have traditionally been addressed by creating "attraction" efforts through the use of financial incentives (such as tax abatements, land write downs and low interest loans) and through agglomeration. Bartik (1991) suggests that there are locales where the use of incentives is appropriate (in places such as economically distressed or high risk areas). He also argues, however, that to use incentives to attract industry to already attractive locations does not make sense.

So if local and state governments should limit their use of financial incentives to attract industry, how should they lure capital and investment? How else could they contribute to the increased creation of wealth and economic development? First, as noted earlier, neither "local" nor "state" governments are well equipped to deal with the issues surrounding regional economies and labor markets. Second, we are in a time of low unemployment and increasing demand for workers, thus offsetting some of the normal "market failure" rationales for government intervention or participation.

The basis for a more proactive policy, we believe, lies in active public-private partnerships. Given the regional nature of the economy, no single governmental entity is able to deal unilaterally with supporting an economic sector's needs and concerns. The Cleveland-Akron CMSA, for example, includes eight counties and numerous local jurisdictions, as well as special state offices and special service districts, thus creating a huge and confusing mosaic of jurisdictions and responsibilities. We argue, therefore, that it is only through partnerships among the private, public, non-profit, educational and philanthropic sectors that a region and its industries continue to maintain a competitive position within a global economy.

The goal of such partnerships would be to position a region to be adaptable and flexible to meet the challenges of the future. Regional economic development policy should not be singularly focused on "market failure" issues but should focus on a "pre-market failure" strategy. Such a strategy would focus on building a flexible and adaptable platform that could accommodate innovation and change, placing the region at or ahead of the curve, rather than waiting for the next change to occur and then attempting to catch up with the competition in a global market. This would require the creation of a flexible and trained workforce, of an entrepreneurial business community, of a "built" and technological infrastructure in place, and of governmental regulations that not only protect the citizenry but also facilitate development and innovation. In short, this means having a region that offers amenities conducive to attracting and retaining both firms and their workers.

The premise behind this research is that regional economic performance (e.g., the quality of jobs, the growth of out-of-region exports, and wealth and income generation) is based on a "portfolio" of industries whose competitive position is reinforced by a network of customers and suppliers. After all, regions are not competitive; only companies and the products they sell can be competitive. A cluster is not simply an alternative term for an industry. Clusters span industries -- and are unique concentrations of interrelated economic activities. By definition, clusters are geographic concentrations of competitive industries that either have close buy-sell relationships, or have common technologies, or share a labor pool that gives businesses within the cluster a competitive advantage. Clusters are centered around the most vital businesses in the region that drive the growth and development of industries which provide services and/or inputs into their operations. An example of an industry cluster is the automobile industry in the Detroit region. All three of the leading American automobile manufacturers are headquartered and maintain production facilities in the Detroit area along with many support companies in the region that supply raw material components and basic services.

REGIONAL CLUSTER-BASED DEVELOPMENT: A CLEVELAND CASE STUDY

This section sketches the central components of a metropolitan Cleveland initiative to foster economic development partnerships and regionalism (based on materials and data taken from Civic Vision, 1998; Greater Cleveland Growth Association, 1997, 1998a & 1998b; Kleinhenz, 1998). This initiative, funded by the Cleveland and the George Gund Foundations, is aimed at understanding the importance of local industry clusters within the regional economy -- assessing how they are performing, investigating the potential of emerging clusters, and providing the analysis needed to support the development of regional economic strategies that strengthen existing clusters and support emerging clusters in Northeast Ohio.

Any regional initiatives must evolve from a partnership of business, governments, non-profits and education/training institutions. In the Cleveland area, a partnership in Northeastern Ohio undertook a project to identify industry "clusters" within the region that were competitive in the global economy. The project, the Northeast Ohio Regional Economic Development Strategies Initiative (NOREDSI), is a partnership of the Akron Regional Development Board or ARDB (the Chamber of Commerce for the Akron area), Cleveland Tomorrow (a committee of the CEO's of the region's largest companies), and the Greater Cleveland Growth Association or GCGA (the Chamber of Commerce for the City of Cleveland). NOREDSI's goal was to promote industrial clusters in the region, so as to become more globally competitive. This initiative sought to generate a bottom-up, private sector program in which interrelated private firms within an identifiable "cluster" could work together to identify and resolve common needs and concerns. This research identified six industry clusters (metalworking, plastic products and chemicals, motor vehicles and equipment, insurance, biomedical products, and instruments and controls) that were relatively competitive or had competitive advantages in the region. In a series of cluster forums with these industries, six main issues were identified by private sector participants as barriers to retaining regional competitive advantages. They were: 1) workforce/education, 2) technology/R&D, 3) entrepreneurship, 4) governmental regulatory and tax policies, 5) quality of life, and 6) infrastructure.

In Northeast Ohio, therefore, the first possible component is in place: consensus about what industry needs to remain competitive in a global market. The next step is a reasoned dialogue with the other providers to convey this information and attempt to reach consensus on how the partners may work together to prepare for the future. The final step is for each partner to implement their programs that will facilitate the creation of a stronger region. The strategic components and policy impacts are described below.

Workforce and Education

In a survey of Northeast Ohio executives, Cleveland State University's Urban Technical Assistance (UTAG) group found that almost 75% of respondents are currently experiencing labor shortages and that nearly 85% expect shortages to continue for at least the next five years. Part of the shortage problem surrounds workers' skill mismatches and workers' being unprepared for current job requirements. These skill mismatches are expected to continue with demands of increasing skill levels in both information and manufacturing technologies. Yet, private sector firms are not investing in incumbent worker training, with almost 50% spending less than the national average of 2% of payroll on training and with another 25% not really sure how much they may be spending. When looking at local universities, one research organization found that the awarding of many critical high technology degrees (i.e., computer science, electrical engineering, engineering technologies, civil engineering and physics) was in decline, at least relative to the United States, between 1985 and 1994. The same study found that in 1997 Cleveland ranked in the third quartile of 36 metro area for percentage of adults with bachelors degrees, as well being in the bottom quartile among 24 metro areas in 1996 for manufacturing workers with some post-secondary education. Obviously, attention must be given to the educational infrastructure to enable the region to be competitive.

If a region is attempting to be globally competitive, a well trained workforce is essential to increasing the levels of productivity. Each school district needs to provide students prepared to enter the labor force. They must possess technological skills (math, science and computer literacy), appropriate social behavior and skills (such as a work ethic, timeliness, dedication, and the ability to work in groups and teams), and the fundamentals of thinking and communication. Without these skills, the region's enterprises will almost inevitably become increasingly uncompetitive in the global environment.

If a region is to be competitive, a number of things may facilitate increasing the levels of education. First, many states are revisiting the constitutionality and/or equity of funding schools through property taxes. While the current funding method in Ohio is under review, a primary concern continues to be intra-regional disparities among communities in both the funding and the quality of education among districts. The City of Cleveland's school district is, by most measures, rated behind most other districts in the region. Yet, it is the largest district in the region and is the one firms look to as a measure of regional educational quality when making location decisions. Cleveland's system is, relative to many neighboring districts, less well funded. It is important that all school districts have relatively equitable funding so that they are able to provide the needed curriculum and standards for a globally competitive region.

To meet skill demands for a globally competitive workplace, school districts need to establish curricula that increase the levels of math, science, and technological literacy. One of the public sector's most vital economic development initiatives, first, is to reach consensus with regional industries on the skill sets needed by firms and, then, to adopt policies ensuring that students can attain them in all districts throughout the region. Next, a common set of standards needs to be in place to establish credentials for the desired skill sets. If students are expected to learn specific skill sets across all districts, employers will need to be confident that the resources to teach these skills are in place. It is essential that some skill-set-based credentials be valid and reliable across the region. In summary, public and private partners need to find ways to fund public education equitably and to provide a common curriculum which is relevant for industry and which can be verified by a common set of evaluations, standards, and credentials.

In a Cleveland State University survey of industry executives, respondents indicated that both public and private universities should "emphasize the 'real world' skills needed in the workplace [such as] computer skills, technical writing, problem solving skills, presentation skills, and basic workplace comport (time management, professional dress, workplace etiquette) [all of which] are sorely lacking among many college educated workers." The report advocates three methods of enhancing these skills through the increased use of internships, externships, and apprenticeships. As a general assumption, industry, as the purchaser of labor, is the true client for educational services rather than the students. As such, one would expect universities and colleges to be responsive to industry's needs, yet this would appear to not be the case.

One proposal to do this was developed by the Economic Growth Working Group (EGWG), a committee of the Northeast Ohio Jobs and Workforce Initiative (JWFI), an organization of private employers which was formed in early 1996 to help the business community focus on workforce development issue. The proposal called for increased funding of chairs and professorships in areas of technology which the region has identified as needed to enhance the core competencies involved in maintaining their competitive advantage. These funded positions would be in the "hard" sciences, such as engineering and computer science. These fields are essential for building capacity within a flexible and adaptable region. These positions would serve a twofold purpose: to train technically proficient graduates and to provide the potential for bringing innovation and technology back to the private sector.

As a general policy, regional economic development officials can help facilitate an agenda for state colleges and universities, as well as for community colleges, to support regional competitiveness. This agenda would build curricula that are based on external demand rather than through institutional turf wars. Institutions of higher education (particularly publicly funded universities, four year colleges and community colleges) need to be more in tune with the needs of industry, especially when training labor in the hard skill areas such as math, sciences, engineering and computers.

Public Entrepreneurship

States have traditionally aided economic development through the supply side, particularly through cost saving types of incentives such as job creation and investment tax credits. In Ohio, as in many other states, the state has worked with both the federal government as well as private industry to establish centers to aid in the development of new processes as well as new products. In Ohio there are eight of these centers, which were launched under the Thomas Edison program. Seven of the centers are targeted to specific industries, such as biotech or polymers; and one, the Cleveland Advanced Manufacturing Program (CAMP), is focused on manufacturing in general. As in many other areas of the "new wave" of economic development, participation on the part of industry comes at a price -- firms are charged a fee for services. Anticipated outcomes for firms are higher productivity, increased sales, lower material and inventory costs, as well as increasing the need for additional workers. While the actual return on investment in the Edison Centers is unknown, the state is currently evaluating the impact of all economic development programs, including the Edison Centers.

The states can help firms to innovate both in process areas and product areas through specialized or regional centers of excellence. Returns to the state can be more competitive industries which retain jobs and expand employment through increased business, as well as through marketing new products. It is also important to note that each Edison Center is located where its industrial base is. In Northeast Ohio, there are the general manufacturing center (CAMP), the Edison Biotech Center (EBTC), and the polymer center (EPIC) in Akron. As part of the on-going clusters work, the biotech cluster, under the auspices of EBTC and the Workforce Initiative, regularly surveys member firms in the biotech, biomedical and bioinformatics industries on the supply and demand of needed skill sets within their industries. The outcomes of the surveys are communicated to local educational institutions, the state Department of Development, and to respondents in the hope of building or importing the critical skill sets needed by these industries both to grow and to remain competitive.

All of the clusters' forums revealed a problem for entrepreneurship in Northeast Ohio: the inability for small business and new product developers to gain access to capital. This is particularly true among people creating products in new and high-tech sectors. The region, unlike Silicon Valley or Boston/128, is unfamiliar with how to make loans for innovations, particularly in the areas of intellectual capital. In advance of the clusters research, a partnership of the Greater Cleveland Growth Association, the Cleveland office of the Small Business Administration (SBA) and the Cleveland Federal Reserve Bank had investigated breakdowns in the lending process to small businesses. This program attempted to replicate research done for the Federal Reserve by Cleveland State University in the area of home mortgage lending. This "access to capital" research produced fourteen recommendations for improving small business access to capital in the region -- five of which are summarized below.

The first recommendation was to form a regional access-to-capital network in which all capital providers and business assistance providers would work together in an easily understood system. Business assistance and advising are provided not only by non-profits, but also by departments of county and local governments. Another recommendation was to create a working capital pool to provide loans from $100,000 to $1,500,000 for short-term periods (less than two years). This would pool capital available from state and local government funding sources, as well as from private lenders and foundations in a "one stop" location. A third recommendation was aimed primarily at the state level: to create a statewide "Access to Capital" (ATC) program. In this area, the state would help to cover losses from loans made to some of the more marginal borrowers. A fourth recommendation suggested developing an ATC database of non-profits, governmental assistance providers, and other funding sources. Included in this would be software designed to help credit seekers to determine worthiness as well as aid in the preparation of loan documents and evidence. State and local resources could be combined into a regional effort to support such information-building efforts. The last relevant part of the report recommended that a regional ATC program needs funding and that local and state governments should be prime participants in providing the funding. If regional ATC "one stops" were in place, work loads for many agencies could be reduced through increased efficiencies. In summary, this initiative advocated that the state and local entities should work together to meet regional needs in access to capital, to help entrepreneurship and small business startups, and to promote product and process innovation and development (Greater Cleveland Growth Association, 1998b).

Technology and R&D Policy

Obviously, investments in technology and R&D efforts are important. Historically, the federal government and private industries funded technology and R&D efforts -- particularly those involving basic research. However, at the regional level industry leaders and university researchers can form partnerships to identify necessary research or to develop and implement emerging technologies which contribute to a cluster's competitive advantage. This may mean investing state and industrial support for basic as well as applied research. Some national models exist for this such as the National Science Foundation's Industry/University Cooperative Research Grant/Center program. Some states have supported technology programs as well -- Ohio's Thomas Edison Program, New Jersey's and New York's Advanced Technology Centers, Pennsylvania's Ben Franklin Partnership, and Texas' Advanced Research Program. Such programs appear to be quite effective. Cohen and his associates (1994) found that state-supported research centers outperformed nationally-funded centers in terms of "commercially oriented" R&D outcomes. Feller and Anderson (1994) found that the cost-benefit ratio contribution to economic development of investments in the New York program to be between three to six times the direct investment of the state -- between $190 million and $360 million.

State policy with respect to technology and R&D should be to encourage and foster partnerships between universities and industry and to identify technology areas which, if developed, would contribute to the competitive advantage of regional clusters. The state could do this by investing in centers of excellence in which R&D ideas could be shared within the clusters (not just between a university and one firm).

Infrastructure Policy

There have been many studies linking the investment in physical infrastructure to economic development (for a review see Arsen, 1997; Felbinger, 1995). Regardless of the figures used to estimate that impact (and they vary quite widely), it is clear that state and local governments need to continue to provide for and regulate the quality of basic infrastructure -- not solely for economic development, but more importantly for the health, safety, and convenience of citizens (Felbinger, 1995). States should continue to fund basic infrastructure and allow regions to identify which systems to support. The state should also act as the convener to plan for and implement new infrastructure systems taking advantage of new technologies, materials, and processes

New construction and regular maintenance should be linked, though, to regional needs. For example, in Ohio decisions regarding state-funded infrastructure investment priorities are made regionally with representatives of each level of government and the private sector at the table. Not only is the decision-making done by virtue of a partnership between government and non-governmental actors, the original initiative and its subsequent reauthorization were championed by a partnership between business leaders and government officials. The business leaders involved specifically linked these investments to the revitalization and restructuring of Ohio's economy.

One aspect of infrastructure, which is often overlooked, is what Felbinger (1995) termed "human infrastructure." Human infrastructure refers to training and enhancing the skills of those who build, maintain, and manage physical infrastructure systems. The vast majority of these people are governmental employees. State and local governments need to maintain the training and development opportunities (and budgets) for their employees. They should also take advantage of technical assistance units within universities. Cities within regions could sponsor joint training efforts. Finally, states can assist cities in purchasing the access to new training delivery mechanisms, such as satellite dishes, telecommunications, and video conferencing.

Tax and Regulatory Policy

State governments should develop and encourage taxing policies which benefit regions. The most commonly used example of tax policy designed to enhance the economic development benefits to a region is Minnesota's shared tax base. Put simply, economic benefits (e.g., taxes) generated by a firm's location in a city in the region accrue to all cities in the region. Of course, the shared tax base plan is more complicated than that and the sharing is not always an even or per capita sharing. However, the point is that the idea of the plan supports the competitive advantage of the region and the notion that partners in the region should not have incentives to steal industries from other partners. Under such a system, cities will not have an incentive to try to "outbid" other cities in the region for the same firm.

On the regulatory side, much has been written in the popular press about easing regulatory pressure on business so as to increase economic development, particularly in an increasingly global environment. That being the case, we offer a somewhat different example of how an examination of current regulations could lead to more innovation and productivity, thus enhancing economic development. Building codes of states and cities may require the use of steel reinforcing bars in non-steel bridges. Research scientists have found that some non-steel composite materials are stronger and last longer than traditional concrete and steel structures. However, as the regulations currently read, the composite material would have to be reinforced. State and local building codes could be more flexible allowing for the adoption of new materials and new processes. This would require that those inspecting the plans (human infrastructure) be up-to-date on the latest science in materials and construction processes. In short, their regulatory codes should be continuously examined to ensure flexibility to meet the needs of a rapidly changing global society.

Amenities and Quality of Life

While amenities are easy to quantify, for example the number of golf courses and beaches and theaters are known, their value and their impact on attracting and retaining firms are difficult to assess. There are numerous anecdotes about how Northeast Ohio has lost or won firms based on the quality or numbers of cultural facilities, sports teams, and sports activities (such as golf courses and boat slips), as well as about the impact of ethnic diversity and climate on the firms' locational decisions. But to quantify the impact and build the "right" group of amenities to attract any targeted firm or industry is done by pure luck. Knox (1997: 21) states that the American cities which are able to compete in the global economy have established "high order cultural amenities" that are available (both to highly paid workers and their out-of-town business visitors).

Basic economics suggest that regions with fewer amenities will need to pay more to attract and retain workers. When considering investment in amenities that can be built or developed, regional consensus and cost sharing should occur. While the new Browns stadium in Cleveland is funded by Cuyahoga County residents, some of the economic and other benefits accrue to the region in general, with a good portion of the population acting as "free riders." In a recent referendum in Pittsburgh to fund a new stadium, voters outside of the central county were asked to share in the costs and benefits of a new stadium; and the voters clearly turned down the referendum.

In looking at any region, attention must be paid to the central city. Although some traditional service sectors have begun to migrate with manufacturing to the periphery, the central business district (CBD) continues, at least in many cases, to be just that, the center of business. It is in a region's interest to maintain a viable urban core. In Cleveland, this has been the role of Civic Vision 2000 and Beyond. This group, composed of representatives from business, government, education and non-profits, has developed a series of ten year plans that envision connecting the downtown and the CBD to the neighborhoods and the region. The plan focuses on redeveloping the lakefront further, creating a downtown convention center, expanding downtown housing, renovating the city's main corridor (Euclid Avenue) from downtown to an area rich in amenities (University Circle); and it also considers the renovation and expansion of existing downtown amenities such as the Cleveland-Cuyahoga Port, parks, and access to the lakefront.

If labor markets continue to be tight, workers will most likely seek, all other things being equal, the nicest places to live and ones that offer the amenities that workers want. Local government can work individually on the smaller and more local amenities, such as pools, parks, and golf courses, but regional work is necessary to provide more highly capitalized amenities, such as stadiums, marinas, and cultural locations with theatres and entertainment districts and venues.

CONCLUSION

If regions (and cities and states in those regions) are to be economically competitive, then they will have to operate in a global environment. Globalization is revolutionizing the economic environment in such a way that innovative strategies of regional cluster-based development are becoming increasingly vital to maintaining or developing economic competitiveness and the prosperity that it brings. The most important contributor to success is not to abandon cities and states as entities. Rather, these entities in both the public and private sectors must understand and act on the concept of an economic region. Within these regions, clustered firms should be willing to share information and technology. Local governments should shed parochial leanings and participate in open partnerships with others (including other cities) in the region. States should be more flexible in easing regulations and opening up more creative financing and taxing mechanisms. The non-profit, foundation, and university communities should be the neutral facilitators of regional thinking. Finally, all of these activities should be focused on establishing creative partnerships for competing in a global environment.

In some ways, this vision suggests the need for a positive revolution in economic development practice. Bingham, Hill, and White (1990) state that economic development is essentially creating jobs and wealth. Bingham and Mier (1993: vii) go further to say that it is the:

> role of the private sector to create wealth by producing tradable goods and services and engaging in these exchanges. It is the role of the public sector to facilitate and promote the creation of jobs and wealth by the private sector, *and to ensure that it does so in a way that serves the short- and long-run interests of the broad population* [emphasis in original].

The central role of human capital in creating and maintaining economic competitiveness under globalization, in turn, means that the social conditions of the "broad population" cannot be ignored, as they generally were in the era of "smoke-stack chasing."

REFERENCES

Arsen, D. 1997. "Is There Really an Infrastructure/Economic Development Link?" pp. 82-98 in R.D. Bingham and R. Mier, Eds., *Dilemmas of Urban Economic Development: Issues in Theory and Practice*. Thousand Oaks, CA: Sage.

Bartelt, D.W. 1997. "Urban Housing in an Era of Global Capital." *The Annals of the American Academy of Political and Social Science* 551: 121-136.

Bartik T.J. 1991. *Who Benefits from State and Local Economic Development Policies?* Kalamazoo, MI: W.E. Upjohn Institute for Employment Research.

Bashi, V.I. and M. Hughes. 1997. "Globalization and Residential Segregation by Race." *The Annals of the American Academy of Political and Social Science* 551: 105-120.

Bingham, R.D., E.W. Hill, and S.B. White. 1990. "Preface," pp. 7-9 in R.D. Bingham, E.W. Hill, and S.B. White, Eds., *Financing Economic Development: An Institutional Response.* Thousand Oaks, CA: Sage.

Bingham, R.D. and R. Mier. 1993. "Preface," pp. vi-xvi in R.D. Bingham and R. Mier, Eds., *Theories of Local Economic Development: Perspectives from Across the Disciplines.* Thousand Oaks, CA: Sage.

Civic Vision 2000 and Beyond. 1998. *Building an Even Greater Cleveland, Volume I: An Overview.* Cleveland: Civic Vision.

Clarke, S.E. and G.L. Gaile. 1998. *The Work of Cities.* Minneapolis: University of Minnesota Press.

Cohen, W., R. Florida, and R. Goe. 1994. *University Industry Research Centers in the United States.* Pittsburgh: Carnegie-Mellon University Press.

Dimitriadis, G. and G. Kamberelis. 1997. "Shifting Terrains: Mapping Education Within a Global Landscape." *The Annals of the American Academy of Political and Social Science* 551: 137-150.

Felbinger, C.L. 1995. "Conditions of Confusion and Conflict: Rethinking the Infrastructure-Economic Development Linkage," pp. 103-137 in D.C. Perry, Ed., *Building the Public City: The Politics, Governance, and Finance of Public Infrastructure.* Thousand Oaks, CA: Sage.

Feller, I. and G. Anderson. 1994. "A Benefit-Cost Analysis of State Technology Development Programs." *Economic Development Quarterly* 8: 127-140.

Greater Cleveland Growth Association. 1997. *Jobs and Workforce Initiative.* Cleveland: Greater Cleveland Growth Association.

Greater Cleveland Growth Association. 1998a. *Accelerating Regional.* Cleveland: Greater Cleveland Growth Association.

Greater Cleveland Growth Association. 1998b. *Access to Capital: A System of Connecting Those Who Need Capital With Those Who Have It.* Cleveland: Greater Cleveland Growth Association.

Haynes, K.E. and R.R. Stough. 1997. "The Federal Urban Policy Agenda: Recent Past and New Realities." *The Annals of the American Academy of Political and Social Science* 551: 73-88.

Kleinhenz, J. 1998. "Cluster Based Economic Development," in a special section "Regionalism 1998." *Northern Ohio Live* 6: (January).

Knox, P.L. 1997. "Globalization and Urban Economic Change." *The Annals of the American Academy of Political and Social Science* 551: 17-27.

Mander, J. 1996. "Facing the Rising Tide," pp. 3-19 in J. Mander and E. Goldsmith, Eds., *The Case Against the Global Economy: And a Turn Toward the Local.* San Francisco: Sierra Club Books.

Schumpeter, J.A. 1983. *Theories of Economic Development.* New Brunswick, NJ: Transaction Books.

Wilson, D. 1997. "Preface." *The Annals of the American Academy of Political and Social Science* 551: 8-16.

Chapter 5

GLOBALIZATION, THE "NEW ECONOMY," AND THE ECONOMIC PERFORMANCE OF THE AMERICAN STATES

Cal Clark and Richard Larkin

Globalization has set off what might be termed "schizophrenic scenarios" (Clark, 2001) in the United States (and world wide) in the sense that there clearly have been winners and losers in the accompanying economic and social change. On the one hand, the loss of unionized manufacturing jobs has devastated families and communities; on the other, the high tech and dotcom revolutions have spawned many entrepreneurial millionaires and created numerous high paying jobs. In particular, areas and individuals who can take advantage of the so-called "new economy" that is based on information technologies and advanced services are presumed to have prospered, while those that cannot are seemingly consigned to economic decline and increasing privation.

The validity of this stereotype about the "new economy" would seem to be of vital importance for economic development policy. If the "new economy" represents a "future that works," states and communities would be foolhardy not to make developing the foundation for such an economy their utmost priority. Conversely, if the "new economy" turns out to be just a trendy buzzword with little developmental impact, restructuring efforts could well turn out to be a costly chase for a chimera. This chapter, hence, examines the impact of the "new economy" upon the economic performance of the American states. It begins by briefly sketching a model of the "new economy" and how it is presumed to differ from the advanced industrial one that has marked U.S. society during the postwar era. The second section describes the central components of a broad-based indicator of how developed this "new economy" is in each of the 50 states. Statistical analysis then tests the association between a state's score on this index and its long-term economic growth rate for 1980-1995.

GLOBALIZATION AND THE EMERGENCE OF THE "NEW ECONOMY"

The general image of the "new economy" is one in which high tech industries and advanced services have replaced traditional manufacturing, especially the "smoke stacks" of heavy industry, as the center of economic activity and dynamism in the United States. The processes of globalization, in turn, are seen as constituting the central force that is producing this huge transformation in America's political economy. Globalization -- that is, the substantial growth of interlinkages among nations and societies, particularly in the economic realm -- is generally considered a process of the postwar era that "took off" in the early 1980s, although important aspects of it can be dated back to at least the 1960s. Two important causes for globalization should be distinguished. First, the transportation and communications revolutions of the second half of the century have made it possible to ship goods, funds, and information around the world cheaply and quickly (Greider, 1997; Thurow, 1992). By themselves, though, these technological changes would not have created an integrated global economy. Consequently, a "second" revolution was vital as well. This is that national borders have become much more porous to economic transactions as part of the U.S.-led efforts at creating a free-trade global economy (Gilpin, 1987), creating what Kenichi Ohmae (1990) has called a "borderless world."

Globalization, in turn, has exerted a rapidly growing impact upon national economies which can be conceptualized in terms of what has been called the "international product cycle." In essence, the international product cycle refers to the life cycle of a particular good or product. Generally, new products are developed and produced in the most advanced industrial nations because they involve the latest (and most expensive) technologies, are produced by very capital-intensive processes, and require highly skilled production workers. Over time, however, the production of the item becomes more standardized and labor-intensive. Consequently, as an industry (e.g., textiles and apparel) "matures" so that production becomes highly standardized and requires only semi-skilled labor, the product cycle works to diffuse its production to countries that are not so technologically advanced but which have lower labor costs and standards of living. Up through World War II, this process was generally confined to Western Europe, North America, and Japan. However, once capital and technology began to spread around the world more rapidly after World War II, an ever accelerating diffusion of production commenced, first to other industrialized countries and ultimately to nations with semi-skilled low-cost labor, thus explaining Third World industrialization and the growing competition faced by mature economies (Gilpin, 1987).

Until quite recently, the implications of this theory for the future of advanced industrial societies, such as the United States, were considered somewhat doleful. Industry and manufacturing were generally seen as creating much higher productivity than other economic activities, such as agriculture and services. Thus, industrialization should make a nation much more prosperous, but this logic also implies that the transformation of an industrial economy to a service-based tertiary one should lead to declining productivity gains and, hence, slower growth (Rostow, 1960). Indeed, the U.S. recession of the early 1990s evoked significant fears that America was experiencing "de-industrialization" that would inevitably create greater poverty and inequality (Greider,

1997; Harrison and Bluestone, 1988; Reich, 1991). However (and fortunately for the U.S.), the recent surge in the high tech and information industries has led to the argument that these new technologies have generated a new upswing in productivity and growth that has been labeled the "new economy." Indeed, productivity surged in America during the second half of the 1990s, bringing with it sustained and rapid growth and a new theory that the Information Age, just like the Industrial Age before it, would create the material basis for rapid growth and prolonged prosperity (Atkinson, et. al., 2000; Friedman, 1999; Thurow, 1999).

This replacement of America's Industrial Age economy by an Information Age one brings to mind Joseph Schumpeter's (1950) critical insight that economic development is a process of "creative destruction." On the one hand, the emergence of the "new economy" represents extremely good news for America. There is "life after manufacturing;" and the very strong performance of the U.S. economy for most of the 1990s demonstrates the vitality and growth of these new industries. Still, there most certainly is an "on the other hand" since the "destructive" half of creative destruction is far too great to be ignored either. Many workers and communities that prospered in the industrial age have proved incapable of adjusting to the "new economy," creating increasing social and economic inequality for a significant segment of the population (Greider, 1997; Harrison and Bluestone, 1988; Thurow, 1996). Given the rapidly diverging fortunes of the new "Silicon Valleys" and the old "rustbelts," therefore, it certainly makes sense to search for the characteristics of and requisites for a successful "new economy." If these can be found, the implications for state and local economic development policy would seemingly be profound.

The problems attendant on the transformation from an Industrial Age economy to the emerging Information Age one are exacerbated because the nature of economic activities is changing fundamentally, generating new types of firms and workers while making the existing ones obsolete. Edward Malecki (1997), for instance, argues that today technology, broadly defined as all forms of knowledge, is the major factor influencing economic development. Lester Thurow (1999) echoes Malecki and contends that control of knowledge has replaced control of natural resources as the new foundation of economic success. According to Thurow (1999: xv), "Knowledge is the new basis for wealth."

This shift from a resource-based to a knowledge-based economy has changed the roles of individual economic actors and the organizational setting in which they perform. Larkin and Lankford (2000) drew upon the work of Atkinson and his associates (2000) to examine the changing realities for individuals and organizations in the "new economy." They concluded, as summarized in Figure 5.1, that the basic organizational building blocks of the old economy were single firms operating in a relatively stable environment, both internally and externally. America was the world leader in mass production that resulted in medium-quality goods at moderate costs. Firms had hierarchical management structures and tended to have adversarial relations with other firms, labor, and government. The processes of globalization, however, are now destroying the U.S.'s comparative advantage in mass production industries at a rapid rate as newly industrializing countries (NICs) are coming to dominate standardized manufacturing based on their very low labor costs.

Figure 5.1: Changing Enterprise Characteristics in the New Economy

Characteristic	Industrial Age Old Economy	Information Age New Economy
Key Economic Actors	Single Firms	Networks of Firms
Firm Structure	Hierarchic, Vertical & Bureaucratic	Network, Horizontal & Entrpreneurial
Management Style	Command & Control	Coordination & Cooperation
Task Orientation	Repetitive	Project Specific
Planning	Reactive	Proactive
Employee Development	Internal	External
Environment	Stable	Dynamic
Staffing Mores	Competitive	Shared Human Capital
Compensation	Salaried Linear	Contracted Non-Linear
Human Resource Needs	Labor	Talent & Skills
Time Frame	Long-term	Short-term
Markets	Stable	Dynamic
Competitive Scope	National	Global
Geographic Mobility	Low	High
Production Technique	Mass Production	Flexible Production
Key Factors of Production	Capital & Labor	Innovation, Quality, Time-to-Market & Cost
Competitive Advantage	Lower Cost through Economies of Scale	Innovation, Quality, Time-to-Market & Cost
Importance of Innovation/Research	Moderate	High
Relations with Firms	Go It Alone	Alliances
Relations with Labor	Adversarial	Collaborative
Relations with Government	Government Impositions	Government Assistance

The "new economy," in contrast, is based on high quality goods and advanced services that require a much different form of organization. In particular, a fundamental transformation from mass production to "flexible production" is well underway. Flexible production involves using highly skilled and motivated workers (unlike the deskilled "drone workers" of mass production) to improve quality and flexibility (Harrison, 1994; Piore and Sabel, 1984; Thurow, 1992; Womack, et al., 1990). Obviously, the rise of flexible production has brought almost revolutionary change to corporate structures. Externally, firms face a far more dynamic and threatening environment; and, as a response to growing risk, a new organizational form is emerging in which networks or alliances of firms are created. Internally, hierarchy is being radically reduced. Flexible production requires skilled and autonomous employees, who are generally paid quite highly. Thus, it has been heralded as a management revolution that "reinvents" the corporation by transferring power downward and making even production work creative and rewarding, but also critically raising the importance of human capital for the work force (see Figure 5.2). Many American corporations have, in fact, responded to competitiveness challenges by taking what Bennett Harrison (1994) calls the "high road" of flexible production, not just high tech firms like Motorola or Intel, but corporations, such as Proctor & Gamble and Rubbermaid whose products seem quite pedestrian (Collins and Porras, 1994; Harrison, 1994; Kanter, 1995; Kash, 1989; Rhinesmith, 1996; Smith, 1995; Waterman, 1994).

Figure 5.2: Changing Characteristics of Workers in the New Economy

Characteristic	Industrial Age Old Economy	Information Age New Economy
Employee Self Concept	Firm Specific	Occupation Specific
Skills	Job-Specific	Broad Skills & Cross Training
Requisite Education	A Skill	Lifelong Learning
Employment	Stable	Marked by Risk & Opportunity
Tenure	Life-long	Temporary
Time Frame	Long-term	Short-term
Self Development	Internal by Organization	External by Employee
Goal	Employment	Higher Income
Labor-Management Relations	Adversarial	Collaborative

MEASURING THE DEVELOPMENT OF THE "NEW ECONOMY"

A sophisticated indicator of how highly developed this "new economy" is in each of the 50 American state has been developed by the Progressive Policy Institute (Atkinson, et al., 2000). This scale is based upon 17 specific indicators of a state's economy that measure a variety of dimensions generally associated with the "new economy." As summarized in Figure 5.3, the scale developed by the Progressive Policy Institute has five major dimensions. However, one of these (economic dynamism) is quite likely itself to be a facet of economic growth. Since we are examining the relationship between the "new economy" and economic growth, we modified the overall index by eliminating this dimension in order to ensure that the observed correlation between these two items is not inflated artificially by including a common factor in each.

Figure 5.3: Components of New Economy Index

Knowledge Jobs
1. Percent of workforce with office jobs
2. Percent of workforce in managerial, technical, and professional jobs
3. Educational level of workforce

Globalization
4. Percent of manufacturing production exported
5. Percent of jobs in foreign-owned companies

Economic Dynamism
6. Percent of jobs in "gazelle" firms (companies with sales growth of 20% for at least four years)
7. "Job churning" (business start-ups plus failures as a percentage of all companies)
8. IPOS (initial public offerings as a percentage of gross state product)

Digital Economy
9. Percent of adults on-line
10. Internet domain names per firm
11. Extent of information technology in K-12 schools
12. Extent of digital technology used in delivery of state government services

Innovative Capacity
13. Percent of jobs in high technology
14. Scientists and engineers as percentage of workforce
15. Number of patents per 1,000 workers
16. Industry R&D spending percentage of gross state product
17. Venture capital investment percentage of gross state product

Sum of Variable "Weights" in Each Dimension

Knowledge Jobs	2.5
Globalization	2
Economic Dynamism	3
Digital Economy	4
Innovative Capacity	4
TOTAL	15.5

Source: Atkinson, Court, and Ward. 2000.

Probably the overriding image of the new economy is that it is based on the high tech industry, involves the widespread utilization of computers and the internet, and relies upon the personnel whom Peter Drucker (1989) has termed "knowledge workers." As listed in Figure 5.3, three of the five dimensions utilized to create the index of a "new economy" are based on these factors. First, the role of knowledge workers in a state's economy is measured by the importance of these occupations in the state's economy and by the educational level of the workforce. Second, the extent of a state's digital economy is measured by the utilization of digital technologies by individuals, companies, schools, and state government. Third, the index includes a dimension of business's "innovative capacity" that is closely linked to its high tech capabilities as measured by the importance of the high tech industry for the state and by corporate emphasis on research and development or R & D. The other two dimensions also tap factors that are widely considered to be closely associated with the "new economy." One is how globalized a state's economy is as measured by the importance of exports and foreign subsidiaries for the state's economy. Finally, the index also includes three measures of economic dynamism, especially in the high tech sector (Atkinson, et al., 2000).

These 17 indicators are measured in a variety of ways and metrics. Therefore, to create a common metric for the overall scale, the raw values on each indicator were converted to a measure of how many standard deviations above or below the mean each state's value for a particular indicator was. These "standardized scores" were then transformed to make them all positive (by adding six to each one); and the resulting values were summed for the indicators in each of the five dimensions or categories. These additive scores for each category were further standardized by dividing each state's score by the score of the highest state to create an index with 100 as the highest score. The final "new economy" index was calculated by taking the average of a state's scores on the five dimension modified by the weighting factor for each dimension listed in Figure 5.3 (some variables were weighted as less than one to prevent highly correlated indicators from biasing the index, so that the weights for the "knowledge jobs" and "innovative capacity" dimensions are less than their number of indicators). For example, Massachusetts has scores of 100 on knowledge workers, 71 on globalization, 62 on economic dynamism, 72 on digitalization, and 100 on innovation, creating a "weighted average" of 82, the highest score among the American states (Atkinson, et al., 2000).

Since we needed to remove the economic dynamism dimension from the index, we used the weighting factors to create a new index of "Nongrowth-related new economy" according to the following formula:

NGNE = ((15.5 x NE) - (3 x ED)) / 12.5

Where:

      NGNE is a state's score on the "NonGrowth-Related New Economy" Index

      NE is its score on the overall "New Economy" Index

      ED is its score on the "Economic Dynamism" Dimension

Weighting factors:

      15.5 is the sum of the weighting factors for all 5 dimensions

      3 is the weighting factor for the Economic Dynamism dimension

      12.5 is the sum of the weighting factors for the other four dimensions

Table 5.1 presents the scores for the fifty American states on both the overall "New Economy" index and for the "NonGrowth-Related New Economy" index. The states along the Pacific coast (Washington, California, and Oregon) and Northeast (Massachusetts, Connecticut, Delaware, New Hampshire, Maryland, and New Jersey) predominate among those with the most developed "new economies," while many of the states in the Mountains and Plains West (Nevada, Wyoming, Iowa, South Dakota, Montana, Oklahoma and North Dakota) and the South (Kentucky, Alabama, Louisiana, Arkansas, and Mississippi) tend to be the weakest in the development of the "new economy." In addition, the "rustbelt" states (Pennsylvania, Ohio, Michigan, Indiana, Illinois, and Wisconsin) have only average scores at best, indicating that the old industrial leaders are certainly not providing the major impetus for America's latest growth spurt.

The descriptive statistics that are reported in the top segment of Table 5.2 show that both distributions approximate normality with most of the cases clustering around the averages (means) of 48 for the overall index and 46.5 for the NonGrowth-Related scale with ten or so states each having fairly high or fairly low scores. The rankings and scores for most states are quite similar on the two scales, as indicated by the correlation coefficients for their association in the middle segment of Table 5.2. The correlation between the absolute values of the two sets of scores is extremely high (Pearson's r = .97), as is the correlation between their ranks (Spearman's rho = .95). Yet, despite the fact that the two scales correspond so closely to one another, removing the "economic dynamism" dimension is clearly warranted when seeking to estimate the relationship between long-term economic growth (1980-95) and the extent to which a state has developed a "new economy" because the "economic dynamism" subdimension is related to growth rate significantly more than four dimensions that compose the NonGrowth-Related New Economy index: the bottom segment of Table 5.2 shows that r = .58 for the former and .38 for the latter.

THE "NEW ECONOMY" AND ECONOMIC GROWTH IN THE AMERICAN STATES

The theory of the "new economy" argues that the forces of globalization have accelerated both the growth of Information Age industries in the U.S. and the loss of traditional standardized manufacturing to "off shore" producers and competitors. This stereotype implies that areas and communities that have adapted to the "new economy" should flourish, while those that remain mired in the past will suffer the consequences. Since (as the index of the "new economy" described in the last section showed) the American states vary considerably in their adaptation, one would predict that the new economy scale would be positively associated with the recent growth (i.e., economic performance) of the states. This section tests this hypothesis and finds very strong support for it.

Table 5.1: State Ratings on "New Economy" Index

State	Overall Index		NonGrowth-Related Index	
	Score	Rank	Score	Rank
Massachusetts	82.27	1	87.18	1
Washington	68.99	4	71.58	2
California	74.25	2	71.12	3
Colorado	72.32	3	68.95	4
Connecticut	64.89	5	65.63	5
Alaska	57.70	13	65.44	6
Delaware	59.87	9	64.64	7
New Hampshire	62.45	7	62.82	8
Minnesota	56.53	14	61.15	9
Utah	63.98	6	60.57	10
Maryland	59.16	11	60.05	11
New Jersey	60.86	8	58.23	12
Virginia	58.76	12	56.28	13
Arizona	59.23	10	53.15	14
Oregon	56.10	15	52.98	15
New York	54.48	16	52.94	16
Vermont	51.87	18	51.45	17
Hawaii	46.14	26	50.23	18
Texas	52.31	17	47.85	19
Rhode Island	45.31	29	47.46	20
Michigan	44.59	34	46.56	21
Pennsylvania	46.72	24	46.15	22
Illinois	48.37	22	46.02	23
Florida	50.75	20	45.48	24
North Carolina	45.16	30	44.43	25
Idaho	47.93	23	44.16	26
Kansas	45.18	27	44.14	27
Ohio	44.74	33	43.73	28
New Mexico	51.43	19	43.70	29
Wisconsin	44.92	32	43.05	30
Tennessee	45.14	31	42.45	31
Missouri	44.24	35	42.42	32
Georgia	46.61	25	41.87	33
Nebraska	41.81	36	41.37	34
South Carolina	39.69	38	40.71	35
Maine	45.62	28	40.42	36
Indiana	40.95	37	39.87	37
Nevada	49.03	21	36.80	38
Wyoming	34.49	41	36.00	39

State	Overall Index		NonGrowth-Related Index	
	Score	Rank	Score	Rank
Iowa	33.51	42	35.66	40
Kentucky	39.40	39	34.02	41
South Dakota	32.33	43	32.45	42
Montana	28.98	46	29.83	43
Oklahoma	38.63	40	29.79	44
Alabama	32.28	44	28.90	45
North Dakota	28.99	45	26.78	46
West Virginia	26.79	48	26.46	47
Louisiana	28.22	47	25.61	48
Arkansas	26.22	49	19.20	49
Mississippi	22.63	50	18.46	50

Source: Atkinson, Court, and Ward. 2000.

Table 5.2: Summary Statistics about the Two Indices

I. Descriptive Statistics about the Distributions

State	Overall Index	NonGrowth-Related Index
Mean	48.07	46.46
Median	46.37	44.24
StandardDeviation	13.26	14.53
Skewness	.26*	-.08*
Kurtosis	.38*	.18*

*Not different from zero to a statistically significant extent

II. Correlation between Two Indices

Absolute values	Pearson's r = .97
Rank Orders	Spearman's rho = .95

III. Correlations of Economic Growth with Indices of New Economy

	Real Economic Growth 1980-95
Score on Economic Dynamism Scale	r = .58
Overall Index of New Economy	r = .49
NonGrowth-Related Index of New Economy	r = .38

THE DIRECT ASSOCIATION BETWEEN THE DEVELOPMENT OF A "NEW ECONOMY" AND ECONOMIC GROWTH

The economic performance of the states is measured by their real annual economic growth over the period of 1980 through 1995. This includes both the economic downturns in the early 1980s and early 1990s and the robust growth that occurred during most of the 1980s and after 1992. Thus, it should be a good measure of the long-term performance of the state economies since brief idiosyncratic surges and drops should not affect the average for a sixteen-year period very much. Table 5.3 presents a ranking of the states in terms of annual growth rates along with their scores on the "new economy" scale. Clearly, the states varied greatly in economic dynamism. Fifteen had robust growth of 3% or more a year, while another fifteen averaged less than 2.0%. Furthermore, the relative development of a "new economy" does appear to have some association with economic growth, albeit not an overwhelming one. The states with the lowest growth, for example, score below the average or mean of 46 on the new economy index; and the very worst performers stand out for their lack of development of a "new economy." In contrast, though, the states with the best economic performance do not, as a whole, score particularly well on the NonGrowth-Related New Economy index. For example, only one of the four states with growth rates of 4% a year and 8 of the 15 with growth rates of 3% a year scored above average in terms of having a "new economy."

Such eyeballing of the data is, of course, rather imprecise. Figure 5.4, therefore, reports the results of a linear regression analysis of the relationship between the long-term growth rate and the development of a new economy, including a scatterplot of the relationship with the regression line and the principal regression statistics. The relationship is perhaps even stronger than was suggested by just eyeballing the data in Table 5.3 or how far individual states fall from the scattergram in Figure 5.4. The overall correlation (Pierson's r) is .38 which is highly significant statistically; and the r^2 of .14 shows that the two variables "share" 14% of their variance. The nature of the two variables makes it questionable to assert that a well developed "new economy" causes growth since it is measured at the end of the temporal growth trend (to be able to confer causality, states with the most developed "new economies" in the early 1980s would have had to have had the highest growth rates over the 1980s and 1990s; unfortunately, data are not available that would allow a test of this hypothesis). Still, this moderate correlation does confirm the premise or hypothesis that states with well developed new economies are reaping the rewards for "creation," while those that have not been able to adjust are facing the ill winds of "destruction."

Table 5.3: State Rankings on Economic Growth and "New Economy" Index

State	1980-1995 Growth Rate	NonGrowth-Related Index
Nevada	5.3%	36.80
Arizona	4.2%	53.15
Georgia	4.2%	41.87
Florida	4.1%	45.48
New Hampshire	3.8%	62.82
North Carolina	3.7%	44.43
Utah	3.4%	60.57
Delaware	3.3%	64.64
Virginia	3.3%	56.28
Tennessee	3.2%	42.45
South Carolina	3.1%	40.71
Washington	3.1%	71.58
Colorado	3.0%	68.95
Maryland	3.0%	60.05
New Mexico	3.0%	43.70
Vermont	2.9%	51.45
Hawaii	2.8%	50.23
Texas	2.8%	47.85
Connecticut	2.7%	65.63
Massachusetts	2.7%	87.18
New Jersey	2.7%	58.23
Alabama	2.6%	28.90
California	2.6%	71.12
Idaho	2.6%	44.16
Maine	2.6%	40.42
Minnesota	2.5%	61.15
Arkansas	2.4%	19.20
South Dakota	2.4%	32.45
Alaska	2.3%	65.44
Mississippi	2.3%	18.46
New York	2.3%	52.94
Oregon	2.3%	52.98
Rhode Island	2.3%	47.46
Missouri	2.1%	42.42
Kentucky	2.0%	34.02
Indiana	1.9%	39.87
Nebraska	1.9%	41.34
Wisconsin	1.9%	43.05
Kansas	1.8%	44.14
Michigan	1.8%	46.56

Pennsylvania	1.8%	46.15
Illinois	1.7%	46.02
Ohio	1.7%	43.73
North Dakota	1.6%	26.78
Montana	1.5%	29.83
Louisiana	1.3%	25.61
Iowa	1.0%	35.66
Oklahoma	1.0%	29.79
West Virginia	0.8%	26.46
Wyoming	-0.1%	36.00

Figure 5.4: Scatterplot of Economic Growth Rate by "Nongrowth-Related New Economy Index"

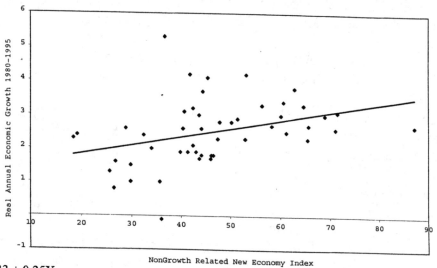

$Y = 1.33 + 0.25X$
$r = .38$
$r^2 = .14$
$t = 2.82$
$Sig = .000$

Adding the Effects of Other Explanatory Factors

Charting the simple or direct association between the new economy index and economic growth is only the first step in examining whether there is an actual relationship between them. Other factors could be just as important, if not more so, in explaining economic performance. Thus, we included three other potential explanatory variables in the analysis. The first is the level of affluence in a state as indicated by its personal income per capita in 1980 at the start of the period under consideration. The second and third independent variables are measures of state government activities in the mid-1980s (near the beginning of the period of growth being measured) that are normally considered antithetical to business activities. One is a sophisticated index of how liberal the policies of a state were that was constructed by Erickson and his associates (1993); and the other is a measure of "tax effort" (roughly the ratio of tax revenues to total personal income in a state) that is used by the Advisory Commission on Intergovernmental Relations (1994).

Figure 5.5 presents the specific hypotheses for how these explanatory factors should affect a state's economic growth rate. The hypotheses for three of the independent variables are straightforward. States that have more highly developed new economies should have higher rates of growth, while those that are more liberal and have higher rates of taxation would be expected have weaker economic performances. In contrast, the expected effect of affluence on growth is ambiguous. On the one hand, richer states should have an advantage because of their past economic success; on the other, they could be held back by their dependence upon existing economic structures in a time of fundamental economic reorientation (see the moderate level of the "new economy" and the low growth rates in the Rustbelt in Tables 5.1 and 5.3, for example).

Figure 5.5: Hypothesized Impact of Explanatory Variables upon Economic Growth Rate

NonGrowth-Related Economy Index*
___
H_1 States with more highly developed "new economies" will have higher rates of growth because they are better equipped for the U.S.'s emerging competitive advantage.

Income per capita
___
H_{2a} More affluent states will have higher growth rates because of the economic advantages that they have accrued in the past.

H_{2b} Less affluent states will have higher growth rates because they can take better advantage of new opportunities for development than states with large "sunk costs" in existing economic structures.

Policy Liberalism
___
H_3 More liberal states will have lower growth rates because liberal policies create an anti-business environment.

Tax Effort
___
H_4 States with higher tax efforts will have lower growth rates because of the disincentives created for business activity.

*Association, not assumed causal impact.

Table 5.4 presents the simple or bivariate correlations among the variables used in this analysis. In terms of the relationships among the independent variables, there appears to be a fairly strong syndrome of strong association among income per capita, policy liberalism, and the development of a NonGrowth-Related New Economy, as the correlations among these three items are all positive and quite strong in the .60 to .68 range. This confirms analyses dating back to Thomas Dye's classic work (1966) that more affluent states and communities have more liberal polil1cies. The advantage that wealthier states have in developing new economies is also far from unexpected. It is certainly interesting, though, to note that policy liberalism has such a strong positive correlation with the development of a new economy. Evidently, more liberal states help business with the development of human capital and, perhaps, technology development, recalling arguments from the 1980s about the efficacy of "industrial policy" (Graham, 1992). This supposition is supported, moreover, by the multiple regression results in Table 5.5 which show that policy liberalism actually has a somewhat stronger impact on the NonGrowth-Related New Economy index (beta = .48) than does state income per capita (beta = .36). Finally, more liberal states exhibit the highest tax efforts with a fairly strong correlation of .54, as would normally be supposed, but tax effort has only a marginally positive association with income per capita and new economy score.

Table 5.4: Correlations Of Economic Growth And "New Economy" Index With Other Explanatory Variables

	Economic Growth Rate	Index of New Economy	Income Per Capita	Tax Effort
NonGrowth-Related New Economy Index	.38**	--		
Income per capita	.03	.65**	--	
Policy Liberalism	-.13	.60**	.68**	--
Tax Effort	-.42**	.15	.28*	.54**

*Statistically significant at .002 level
All correlations are Pearson r's

Table 5.5: Multiple Regression Results Explaining Score on Nongrowth-Related New Economy Index

Overall Equation
R   = .70
R^2 = .50
F   = 14.45
Sig = .000
a   = 28.12

Individual Effects	b	beta	t	Sig
Policy Liberalism	6.98	.48	2.67	.011
Income per capita	0.0023	.36	2.40	.021
Tax Effort	-0.208	-.23	-1.70	.097

Despite the positive correlations among the four independent variables, the hypotheses in Figure 5.5 that predicted different types of impact are generally confirmed. As predicted, the new economy is positively correlated with growth, while both tax effort and political liberalism exhibit negative relationships. That is, growth is lower in states that have higher tax efforts (as indicated by a moderate r of -.42) and more liberal policies, although here the correlation is too small (-.13) to be significant, either statistically or substantively. State affluence has almost no association with economic growth rate, perhaps because the hypothesized positive and negative influences (see Figure 5.5) canceled each other out. These bivariate results, then, solidify our confidence that the new economy is associated with a good economic performance among the states. Its moderately positive correlation is far higher than those for two of the other potential explanatory factors, a state's affluence and political orientations. Tax effort has almost the same degree of association, but is only marginally related (if that) to the degree that a new economy has developed in a state. Thus, it cannot explain or make spurious the observed association between the new economy scale and growth rate.

The last step in the analysis is to apply multiple regression to sort out the individual effects of the four explanatory factors; and these results are reported in Table 5.6. Unfortunately, problems of multicollinearity (i.e., high intercorrelation among the independent variables) forced us to drop political liberalism from the regression equation. The other three independent variables provided an interesting analysis, though. Together, they had a fairly strong combined impact, as indicated by he Multiple R of .64 and explained variance or R^2 of 41%. Since the highest simple correlation was -.42 (see Table 5.4), several of the variables obviously contributed independent and nonoverlapping explanatory power. The individual effects confirm the very significant association between progress toward a new economy and economic growth. In fact, the NonGrowth-Related New Economy index had significantly more influence on growth (beta = .59) than tax effort did (beta = -.45), while income per capita exercised a marginally negative effect as well once the effects of the other independent variables were controlled (beta = -.23).

Table 5.6: Multiple Regression Results Explaining Economic Growth Rate

Overall Equation*
R   = .64
R^2 = .41
F   = 10.47
Sig = .000
a   = 4.77

Individual Effects	b	beta	t	Sig
New Economy	0.040	.59	3.97	.000
Tax Effort	-0.027	-.45	-3.76	.000
Income per capita	-0.0001	-.23	-1.52	.14

*Political liberalism could not be included in the regression equation because of problems of multicollinearity.

THE IMPORTANCE OF THE "NEW ECONOMY:" A WAKE-UP CALL FOR STATE-LOCAL ECONOMIC DEVELOPMENT POLICY?

Our analysis found that the "new economy" appears to be closely tied to how well or ill a state's economy performed over the last two decades. Clearly, a fundamental and far-reaching structural transformation is well underway in the United States; and, just as clearly, some parts of the nation are prospering and some are suffering as a result. This certainly indicates that state and local economic development policy would be well advised to promote the factors that are most closely associated with the "new economy." Schumpeter's (1950) view of "creative destruction" suggests that those who can make the transformation to the "new economy" will live quite well in the early twenty-first century but that those who fail to adapt will face very serious consequences (Friedman, 1999; Smith, 1995; Thurow, 1999).

This conclusion is more than a little ironic, however, in view of recent research findings about state-local economic development policy. In the 1980s, it appeared that many states were reorienting their strategies for promoting economic development from traditional "smoke-stack chasing" to what Clark and Montjoy (1998) have called "upgrading entrepreneurship" which would seem quite congruent with the needs for promoting a "new economy" (Brace, 1993; Clark and Montjoy, 1998; Eisinger, 1988). Unfortunately, the recession of the early 1990s brought smoke-stack chasing back in vogue as state and local officials felt pressured to get quick results on the economic front (Brace, 2001). Hopefully, the economic surge of the 1990s and the rise of the new economy will inspire a new reorientation in many states and localities to put much more emphasis on developing the human capital and socioeconomic infrastructure needed to compete in the "new economy."

REFERENCES

Advisory Commission on Intergovernmental Relations [ACIR]. 1994. *Significant Features of Fiscal Federalism*. Washington, D.C.: U.S. Government Printing Office.

Atkinson, R.D., R.H. Court, and J.M. Ward. 2000. *Technology, Innovation, and New Economy Project*. www.neweconomyindex.org.

Brace, P. 1993. *State Government and Economic Performance*. Baltimore: Johns Hopkins University Press.

Brace, P. 2001. "Mapping Economic Development Policy Change in the American States." *Policy Studies Review* 8:3.

Clark. C. 2001. "Globalization: Schizophrenic Scenarios and the Need for Creative Crossdressing in U.S. Policy," in J. Behar and M. Schoenhals, Eds. *Visions of the 21st Century: Social Research for the Millennium*. New York: New York University Press.

Clark, C. and R. Montjoy. 1998. "Globalization and the Revitalization of U.S. Economic Competitiveness: Implications for Economic Development Policy," pp. 151-182 in K.T. Liou, Ed. *Handbook of Economic Development*. New York: Marcel Dekker.

Collins, J.C. and J. Porras. 1994. *Built to Last: Successful Habits of Visionary Companies*. New York: HarperCollins.

Drucker, P.F. 1989. *The New Realities*. New York: Harper & Row.

Dye, T.R. 1966. *Politics, Economics, and the Public: Policy Outcomes in the American States*. Chicago: Rand McNally.

Eisinger, P.K. 1988. *The Rise of the Entrepreneurial State: State and Local Economic Development Policy in the United States*. Madison: University of Wisconsin Press.

Erikson, R.S., G.C. Wright, and J.P. McIver. 1993. *Statehouse Democracy: Public Opinion and Policy in the American States*. New York: Cambridge University Press.

Friedman, T.L. 1999. *The Lexus and the Olive Tree*. New York: Farrar, Strauss, Giroux.

Gilpin, R. 1987. *The Political Economy of International Relations*. Princeton: Princeton University Press.

Graham, O.L., Jr. 1992. *Losing Time: The Industrial Policy Debate*. Cambridge: Harvard University Press.

Greider, W. 1997. *One World, Ready or Not: The Manic Logic of Global Capitalism*. New York: Simon & Schuster.

Harrison, B. 1994. *Lean and Mean: The Changing Landscape of Corporate Power in the Age of Flexibility*. New York: Basic Books.

Harrison, B. and B. Bluestone. 1988. *The Great U-Turn: Corporate Restructuring and the Polarizing of America*. New York: Basic Books.

Kanter, R.M. 1995. *World Class: Thriving Locally in the Global Economy*. New York: Simon & Schuster.

Kash, D.E. 1989. *Perpetual Innovation: The New World of Competition*. New York: Basic Books.

Larkin, G.R. and W.M. Lankford. 2000. "New Organizational Paradigms for a New Millennium." Session presented at the Annual Organizational Behavior Teaching Conference, Carrollton, GA.

Malecki, E.J. 1997. *Technology & Economic Development: The Dynamics of Local, Regional, and National Competitiveness*, 2nd Ed. Edinburgh Gate, Harlow: Addison Wesley Longman Lmt.

Ohmae, K. 1990. *The Borderless World: Power and Strategy in the International Economy*. New York: Harper Business.

Piore, M.J. and C.F. Sabel. 1984. *The Second Industrial Divide: Possibilities for Prosperity*. New York: Basic Books.

Reich, R.B. 1991. *The Work of Nations: Preparing Ourselves for 21st-Century Capitalism*. New York: Knopf.

Rhinesmith, S.H. 1996. *A Manager's Guide to Globalization: Six Skills for Success in a Changing World*, 2nd Ed. Chicago: Richard D. Irwin.

Rostow, W.W. 1960. *The Stages of Economic Growth: A Non-Communist Manifesto*. Cambridge: Cambridge University Press.

Schumpeter, J.A. 1950. *Capitalism, Socialism, and Democracy*, 3rd Ed. New York: Harper & Row.

Smith, H. 1995. *Rethinking America: A New Game Plan from the American Innovators: Schools, Business, People, Work*. New York: Random House.

Thurow, L. 1992. *Head to Head: The Coming Battle Among Japan, Europe, and America*. New York: Warner.

Thurow, L.C. 1996. *The Future of Capitalism: How Today's Economic Forces Shape Tomorrow's World*. New York: Morrow.

Thurow, L.C. 1999. *Building Wealth: The New Rules for Individuals, Companies, and Nations in a Knowledge-Based Economy*. New York: HarperCollins.

Waterman, R.H., Jr. 1994. *What America Does Right: Lessons from Today's Most Admired Corporate Models*. New York: W.W. Norton.

Womack, J.P., D.T. Jones, and D. Roos. 1990. *The Machine that Changed the World: The Story of Lean Production*. New York: Macmillan.

II. PITFALLS IN A CHANGING UNIVERSE

Economic Development Policy in the American States: Back to an Inglorious Future?

Paul Brace

The American states are at a critical juncture. With the federal government in fiscal and programmatic retreat, political responsibility and authority have become decentralized. The states have developed and implemented new policies for nurturing their economies in a changing economic and political landscape. At the same time, old development strategies linger and many old patterns of economic competition among states persist. Thus, while many important opportunities for change in and the reinvigoration of politics and economics are present, there also exists a threat of dysfunctional competition among political jurisdictions producing insufficient revenues for financing education and infrastructure. Ultimately, this may undermine self-sustained economic development over the long run.

The "new wave" of economic development strategies developed in the 1970s and 1980s produced subtle economic benefits and required concerted effort on the parts of states to maintain because they typically required the investment of state revenues. These strategies, furthermore, could work to price some jurisdictions out of the market for jobs by raising labor costs (Brace, 1993). Old approaches to attracting firms through incentives and subsidies, seldom found to be successful in the long-run, have remained a temptation for politicians seeking options to produce results, even if these results remain largely symbolic or short-sighted.

Economic development activity in the states is currently a frenzied mix. One set of policies is intended to help states target and nurture their economic strengths, while another emphasizes the creation of high-visibility packages to lure large, trophy firms. Where we once wondered if the former were displacing the latter in a new political economy, it now seems clear that both approaches will coexist for some time. An interesting question thus presents itself. Why, despite compelling evidence arguing against their use, do ever-larger incentive packages continue to be offered by the states to attract firms? In addition, we might ask why this tired, old, and seemingly self-defeating approach continues to be pursued even with increasing vigor while more reasoned efforts at developing the productive capacity of the workforce and the infrastructure of states seem to be declining in emphasis if not in numbers?

FUNCTIONAL FEDERALISM AND THE
RISE OF THE ENTREPRENEURIAL STATE

Contemporary economic development policymaking in the American states can best be understood within the changing parameters of American federalism. In the 1950s and 1960s state governments were the "fiscal stepchildren" (Van Horn, 1989) of the federal system. Under that system, what Paul Peterson (1995) labels the legislative model of federalism, federal distributive programs guided most policymaking and expenditures. The major incentives guiding this system were the electoral goals of members of Congress; and rewards were directed toward their constituencies. Development in this era resulted from expenditures on dams, courthouses, museums, atomic colliders, and so forth. There was commonly little concern with how good or bad many of these projects were -- historical monuments to Lawrence Welk and Zane Grey come to mind as extreme examples -- so long as they delivered tangible benefits for which Senators or Representatives could claim credit.

Economic development under this old model of federalism was dominated by federal allocation and was quite haphazard for the most part. The consequences of federal spending did little to offset fiscal inequalities existing among state and local governments. Instead, members of Congress, seeking electoral advantage, added to the burden of state and local governments, inefficiently allocating resources among them (Peterson, 1995: 49). From urban renewal to the war on poverty, the political benefits of pork barrel legislation seemingly outpaced the costs of additional taxation. Consequently, federal grants programs went through extraordinary growth between 1957 and 1977 and resulted in huge allocations of federal dollars. Eisinger (1988: 124) observed that the motives, origins, and actors suggest that "federal action in this area has never been an effort to elaborate or fill out a predetermined economic development policy framework."

Many events can be highlighted as sources of political and economic change in the states (e.g., the depression in the 1930s, redistricting and civil rights legislation in the 1960s). Taxpayer revolts, shifting ideological directions in Washington, fiscal deficits, and budgetary crises placed the conventional pork barrel system under pressure. Of special interest, however, were dramatic fiscal changes. Beginning in the 1960s, the states had to pick up an ever-growing piece of the revenue pie. Furthermore, a certain ambivalence about the federal role in economic development emerged during the Reagan years; and efforts were made to terminate the major remaining federal programs (Eisinger, 1988). The Omnibus Reconciliation Act of 1981 reduced federal aid payments to the states and localities by seven percent, the first cut in constant dollar terms in 25 years (Nathan and Doolittle, 1987). Fortunately, and probably not coincidentally, state capitols became centers of innovation and leadership, rather than politically moribund backwaters (Brace and Ward, 1999; Osborne, 1988; Sabato, 1983). Increasingly, state governments became more able participants in the policymaking process.

Arguably, a different constellation of political and economic interests are being served in the new federalism. The claims of geographically specific interests have less political influence; and economic forces in society are forcing each level of the federal system to focus on issues within its area of competence in this new political-economic federal environment (Peterson, 1995: 83). The primary competence of state and local governments, according to this interpretation, is in development. For many years before this, state and local governments maintained a developmental focus, spending twice as much in these areas as the national government as far back as 1962 (Peterson, 1995: 69). However, as the new political-economy has emerged, this functional differentiation between levels of government has accelerated. The federal government has focused more on redistribution. Subnational jurisdictions are concentrating on the developmental domain. These alternative specializations are not rigidly fixed but, as Thomas Anton (1984) has noted, while the differences in policy interests do not preclude one level from entering the other's sphere of interest, they do help to restrain such entry.

State economic development policies are certainly not new, of course. Initial efforts to attract firms date back to the Balance Agriculture with Industry program initiated by Mississippi. Mississippi sought to lure businesses from the North with offers of cheap and abundant nonunion labor, low-priced land, minimal taxes, and with the then new policy of state-sponsored, tax-exempt industrial-revenue bonds. The results of those early efforts are instructive. Real Silk Hosiery Mills Inc. was the first company to capitalize on these new policies. The Indianapolis-based company was reeling in the midst of the depression and a bitter strike in 1934. Durant, Mississippi, a small job-starved community, issued $25,000 in industrial revenue bonds to buy land and build a facility to lease to Real Silk for $5 per year. Durant also waived five years of county and property taxes, provided insurance, set up a school to train workers, and built housing. In 1946 Durant would issue a $60,000 bond issue to help the plant expand. By the 1950s, however, Real Silk closed all of its facilities across the country, before the first bond was repaid to Durant. Despite this and similar experiences in other states, and despite the fact that Mississippi was dead last economically when it started its economic development strategy and remains dead last over 60 years later, states have relied heavily on this strategy to attract or retain firms.

The older approach to development was joined in the 1970s by more sophisticated state programs focusing not just on getting jobs but on securing good jobs. These programs sought to make states more productive, not just cheaper, places to conduct business (Eisinger, 1988). In the new era of functional federalism (Peterson, 1995) states became less hampered by federal encroachment and were freed or perhaps induced to pursue economic development with ever-growing intensity in the 1980s and 1990s.

At the close of the 1980s, two alternative approaches to economic development were evident in the states. The old approach, which Eisinger (1988) labeled the supply-side strategy, focused on competition to lure employers with subsidies and tax concessions and was primarily interested in increasing the quantity of jobs within states. The other, newer approach, which he labeled the demand-side strategy, emphasized strategic efforts to improve the productive capacity of the states and to improve the quality of jobs within. Where the former strategy emphasized the short-run by using lavish inducements, the latter utilized public funds for investment to produce long-term results.

Some saw the changes occurring in the states as ushering in a new era in development policymaking in the states. However, there were still reasons to question the stability and resilience of these economic development trends. Eisinger (1988: 342) felt these new policies represented the "seeds of a genuine transformation in the American political economy," but he also was very cautious in his interpretation of the magnitude of these changes, describing them as technocratic experiments taking place largely outside of public debate. Viewing the developments in the midst of the recession of the early 1990s, I came to wonder if the fiscal and economic pressures on states would lead them to abandon these experiments in favor of older approaches to development (Brace, 1993). As the 1990s close, we may now assay the major contours of state economic development in the new subnational political economy.

ECONOMIC DEVELOPMENT IN THE EMERGING POLITICAL ECONOMY

Devolution and the emergent political economy have contributed to a functional differentiation of policy responsibility, with the states assuming a heightened role in development. Disciplined by inter-jurisdictional economic competition, they are sensitive to market forces and well-suited and poised to promote economic development (Peterson, 1995). Yet, the incentives currently facing states may also accelerate pressures to engage in competition for jobs and firms with other states (Brace, 1993 & 1997). Just like in the classic prisoners' dilemma, the states may pursue options that are individually rational but collectively sub-optimal. Predatory competition for firms using subsidies and tax abatements may give away far more in fiscal resources than are gained in jobs and growth.

Even a decade ago, there was substantial evidence to suggest that the supply-side approach did little to grow a state's economy. As Peter Eisinger noted (1988: 201):

> Whether or not supply-side inducements are important enough in the calculus of investment to make a difference in drawing firms and capital to a particular place has been of such substantial importance for public policy and at the same time so intractably difficult to answer that it has generated an enormous but finally inconclusive literature.

At best, supply-side initiatives could be viewed as an exercise in symbolic politics in an effort to fashion a hospitable business climate (Eisinger, 1988: 337). Demand-side initiatives required investment and sustaining a multiplicity of programs on a broad front. The tangible consequences of these programs are equally difficult to evaluate; and they may actually hinder job creation by making incomes higher (Brace, 1993). In the end, these more self-conscious programmatic efforts deliver subtle benefits and may be harder to maintain (Brace, 1993).

A Third Wave of demand-side economic development policies was evident beginning as far back as the 1970s as Figure 6.1 makes clear. The strategies were never uniform across states or even constant from year to year within states, but they did share three common elements: 1) improved access to credit, 2) measures to promote exports by state-based firms, and 3) industrial technology programs (Donahue, 1997). States as diverse as Mississippi and New York created venture capital corporations. A majority of states created high-tech development and technical assistance programs to stimulate technological growth. In Michigan, Governor James Blanchard created a Strategic Fund and a Modernization Service, intended to use state financial resources to help the state modernize and diversify its manufacturing base. Massachusetts Governor Michael Dukakis helped initiate an Industrial Service Program to provide state funds intended to distribute growth throughout the state and to provide businesses with capital and services. In New Jersey, Governor James Florio initiated a public works investment program to improve transportation and create 150,000 jobs. By the mid-1980s, all but a handful of states had invested in programs to stimulate foreign trade and market development in some manner.

Figure 6.1 illustrates the explosion in the adoption of many of these types of policies.[1] Some policies (such as those to recruit or retrain industrial employees and state or university assistance to industry) were in place in almost all the states by the early to mid-1970s. Others (such as export promotion, research and development promotion, state development authorities, and state support for training hard core unemployed) proliferated in the late 1970s through the 1980s. It is clear from Figure 6.1 that by 1980 over half of the states had adopted some form of "Third Wave" policy and that by the early 1990s upwards of 80 percent of all the states had adopted most of these forms of economic development policies. Clearly, from a competitive standpoint, there was less and less to differentiate the states on this dimension of economic development policy as we entered the 1990s.

As the economic boom of the 1980s came to a crashing halt, however, so too did the political fortunes of economically innovative and celebrated interventionist governors (e.g., Blanchard, Cuomo, Florio). With the national recession of the 1990s, another era of state political economy has emerged. With the shortfall in revenues resulting from the recession and from the unrelenting pressure of new federal mandates, many states found themselves teetering on the brink of fiscal disaster in the early 1990s. Fifty percent of the states could not fund their fiscal 1992 budget, despite tax increases totaling over $16 billion in fiscal 1991. In this period of fiscal crisis, the pressure to appear to be doing something even symbolically became enormous; and, as we shall see below, new and more aggressive efforts at firm-chasing emerged. Thus, while Third Wave economic

---

[1]The data used in Figures 6.1-6.5 are taken from the *Site Selection Handbook* (various years) and were graciously supplied by Sharon Fox and Laura Langer. The author owes them each a tremendous debt of gratitude.

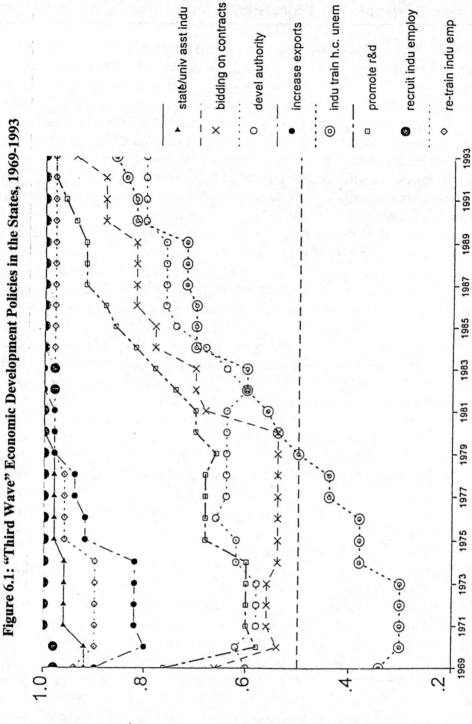

Figure 6.1: "Third Wave" Economic Development Policies in the States, 1969-1993

state/univ asst indu

bidding on contracts

devel authority

increase exports

indu train h.c. unem

promote r&d

recruit indu employ

re-train indu emp

Proportion of States with Specific Economic Development Policies

YEAR

more aggressive efforts at firm-chasing emerged. Thus, while Third Wave economic development efforts have made a mark, they no longer serve as a means for states to get out in front of other states; and they have not supplanted old style approaches, as we shall see.

Despite the ubiquity of Third Wave policies, they are modestly funded with approximately $8 per capita in state and local economic development spending going to such programs (Bartik, 1994). Most of the public resources for economic development go to tax and other financial subsidies in more traditional efforts to encourage firms to locate or expand in a particular governmental jurisdiction (Bartik, 1994). Examples of such subsidies include: property tax abatements, low-interest loans, tax exempt bonds to finance business expansion, wage subsidies, free land, and infrastructure. Reliable statistics on these subsidies are rare. Data on the magnitude of economic development tax expenditures are sparse. Three states compile data. In Michigan, annual revenue foregone through property-tax abatements exceeds $150 million total or over $16 per capita (Citizens Research Council, 1986). New York gave away state and local tax breaks promoting economic development that exceeded $500 million annually (or over $27 per capita) in 1986 (Regan, 1988). In Louisiana, industrial business property-tax exemptions cost over $270 million annually or over $60 per capita. (Schweke, et al., 1994).

Figure 6.2 maps the prevalence of major forms of tax incentives in place in the states. In 1969, fewer than half of the states had corporate, personal income, or excise tax incentive programs. By the mid-1980s, over half of the states had enacted some form of

Figure 6.2: General Tax Incentive Policies in the States 1969-1993

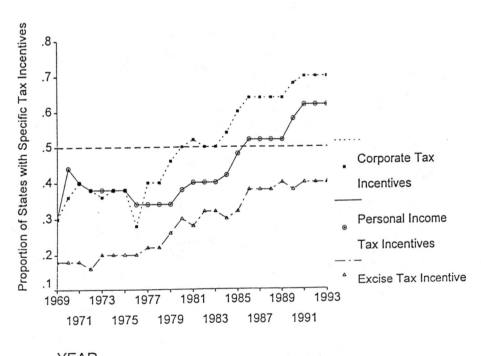

corporate or personal income tax incentive program. A comparatively small minority of states had excise incentive tax programs even in the early 1990s. It is clear from this, however, that most states have moved toward tax incentives as one means to nurture development.

An even clearer picture of the scope of tax incentives can be derived from Figure 6.3 which maps the extent of specific tax incentive adoptions for industry in the same period. Steady growth was evident in the adoption of almost all of these industrial tax incentives with two minor exceptions. Tax exemptions for research and development and accelerated depreciation have been adopted by only a very small number of states. After use in only a handful of states, there was a precipitous jump in the adoption of tax credits for use of specific state products and tax stabilization agreements. By the mid-1980s, a majority of states had adopted 6 of these 8 industrial tax policies. The use of financial incentives to attract business also continued to proliferate through the 1970s and 1980s. As illustrated in Figure 6.4, by the beginning of the 1990s over 80 percent of the states had at least some form of financial incentive package in place.

Figure 6.3: Industrial Tax Incentives in the States 1969-1993

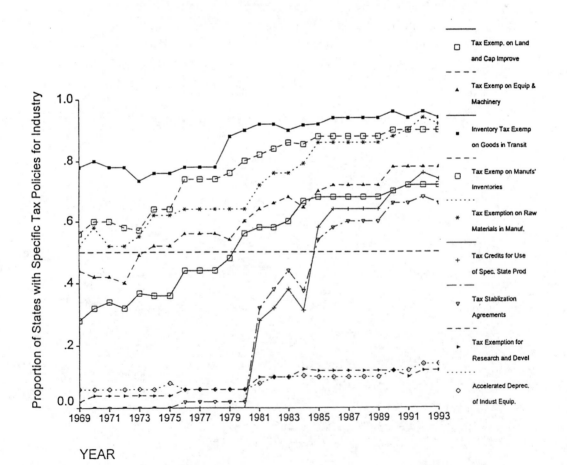

Figure 6.4: Major State Financial Incentives 1970-1990

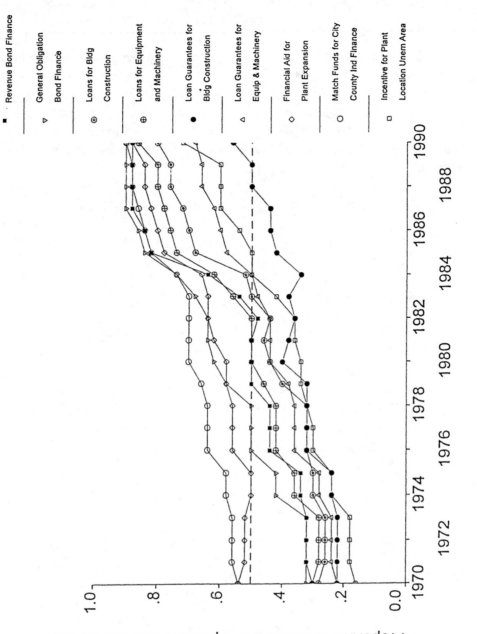

- ■ Revenue Bond Finance
- ▽ General Obligation Bond Finance
- ◎ Loans for Bldg Construction
- ⊕ Loans for Equipment and Machinery
- ● Loan Guarantees for Bldg Construction
- ◁ Loan Guarantees for Equip & Machinery
- ◇ Financial Aid for Plant Expansion
- ○ Match Funds for City County Ind Finance
- □ Incentive for Plant Location Unem Area

Proportion of States with Specific Financial Incentives

YEAR

Just as Figures 6.1-6.4 suggest that the states have been, in general, quite friendly to business, Figure 6.5 indicates that an alternative posture has emerged with regard to organized labor. As this figure reveals, about 40 percent of the states have adopted Fair Employment Practice Codes; and this figure has been almost constant since the late 1960s. Right to Work laws, however, have been adopted by an increasing number of states across this period. By the early 1990s, over half of the states had enacted Right to Work legislation.

Figure 6.5: Labor Policy in the States 1969-1993

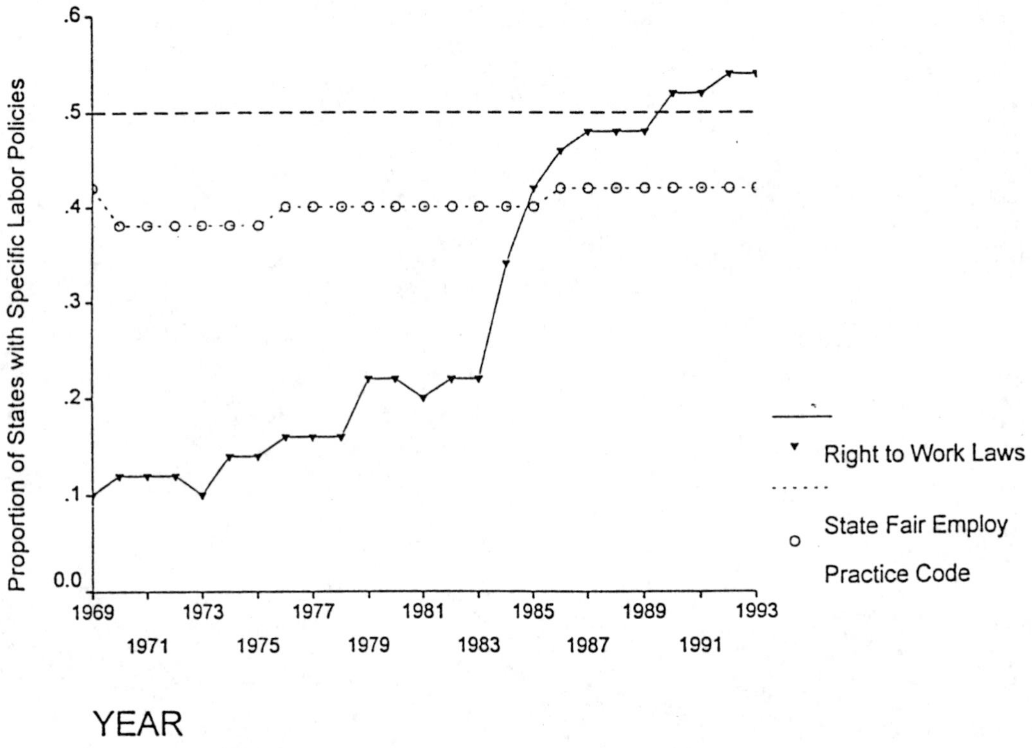

Reviewing Figures 6.1-6.4 highlights a striking pattern evident across the states in economic development policymaking in this era. States adopted a wealth of policies that are business-friendly, either through incentives or various services and infrastructure improvements. Figure 6.5 suggests that many states were also abetting enterprise by adopting a less-labor friendly posture. In sum, there was a remarkable trend toward convergence where by the 1990s most of the states adopted many, if not most, of the major tax and financial incentive policies, along with a substantial number of the "Third Wave" policies; and more rather than fewer states favored the open shop. Thus, by the mid-1990s the business environment offered by most states had become decidedly business friendly -- perhaps too friendly, as we shall see below.

Throughout the 1990s, the most visible efforts in economic development policy efforts have focused on luring major firms to individual states. In the 1980s Japanese auto makers obtained then-record subsidies for new plants in Ohio, Tennessee and Kentucky. Kentucky in 1988 began a 6 percent wage subsidy program for new firms locating in high unemployment counties and has since expanded the geographic scope of this program. Kentucky's aggressive wage subsidy was imitated by Ohio, Oklahoma, Mississippi, and Alabama (Schweke, et al., 1994: 14 & 38). Today roughly 15,000 different agencies compete annually for only 2,400 annual expansions (Freidman, 1996).

More recently, the bidding wars have expanded to include domestic and European firms; and the subsidies have grown astronomically. For example, when United Airlines announced its intention to locate a maintenance facility, a high stake auction among the states resulted. The "winner," the city of Indianapolis, hooked the prize with a bid of $291 million dollars worth of subsidies. The cost per job in this contest worked out to almost $50,000. Northwest Airlines recently secured $270 million in loans from the state of Minnesota to prop up the company's shaky finances. In the automobile industry, South Carolina scored big by luring BMW but not without a large price tag. The state offered Bayerische Motoren Werke AG at least $130 million in incentives to build its factory there and paid to relocate 100 families so the company could have the exact site it wanted, offering to lease the reclaimed land to the prestige automaker for a dollar a year.

Mercedes Benz and Alabama quickly took the bidding to a new plateau. The initial disclosure of $253 million in incentives to attract the 1,500 jobs offered by Benz was later revealed to be a $325 million package. Some of the incentives were symbolic. Alabama officials agreed to place the Mercedes emblem atop a local scoreboard in time for the big, nationally televised Tennessee-Alabama football game at no charge to the company. Mercedes, furthermore, was designated the official automobile of the state of Alabama; and the state has agreed to purchase not less than 100 of the company's new sport utility vehicles, with a ten-year commitment to purchase 2,500 vehicles. The financial core of the deal was very serious business, however. Among the incentives were commitments by the state to spend $1.5 million per year for five years on image advertising and public relations promoting Mercedes' decision to locate in Alabama; to contribute $5 million to Mercedes if it decided to build a visitor's center; to make the U.S. Navy port at the Alabama State Docks available to Mercedes if it decided to ship cars through the port of Mobile; to build a $30 million permanent training center at the plant site, as well as contributing $5 million a year toward the center's operation; to extend a tax-credit available in advance in the form of an interest free loan; and to make an additional $60 million available to educate and train Mercedes employees, including sending people to Germany to study at the company's headquarters (Brace, 1997).

A final episode can further illustrate the downside of these efforts. Rio Rancho, New Mexico, one of the nation's fastest growing cities, made headlines when it beat cities in Oregon, California, Texas and Arizona to become the new home of a $1 billion Intel semiconductor plant. Intel presented prospective communities with its 104 point "ideal incentive matrix" which included tax, utility and workforce subsidies, and regulatory relief. With its $114 million dollar package, Rio Rancho was the "winner" but victory wasn't so sweet. The aquifer in the community wasn't sufficient to satisfy Intel's needs.

Noxious pollution traced to the plant began to cause skin disorders among residents. The community was unable to pay for essential public services including schools for the children of the families lured to the community. They would eventually seek education support from the state legislature parading children wearing "We're desperate" ribbons (Freidman, 1996).

Even though the best evidence would seem to suggest that most high-quality jobs are produced by small to midsize companies, subsidy battles seem skewed in favor of the larger companies that are capable of mounting large and continuous lobbying campaigns. Unfortunately, the subsidies given to large firms may do the most harm to these smaller firms that rely heavily on state education, training and transportation programs. Ultimately, these subsidy battles may create a *surfeit of private goods* (Burstein and Rolnick, 1995). According to this interpretation, economic development competition is a classic collective action problem (see Brace, 1993 for a similar discussion). Collectively, the nation is hurt by irresponsible subsidies because they commonly cause states or communities to misallocate their total resources, neglecting the appropriate mix of public goods that could include state support for such things as education, roads and communication, while instead fixating on wooing the private sector. Money spent on public goods can complement private development but when those funds are instead used to pay individual firms, the state loses in the long-run (Burstein and Rolnick, 1995). Yet these policies persist because the incentives operating on the states individually do not necessarily produce desired or optimal outcomes collectively.

THE GROWING COST OF THE "FREE" MARKET

A critical feature of these efforts is illustrated in Figure 6.6[2] which depicts the well known rise in the per job costs of some prominent subsidy packages. There has been an extraordinary escalation in the amount of resources states are willing to confer on firms to get them to re-locate or remain. Since the 1970s, the cost per job some states have been willing to pay has increased over ten-fold. As the simple regression of these non-randomly selected examples illustrates, the cost per job has risen between $14,000 and $15,000 per year over the period.

There is evidence, furthermore, that firms are taking subsidies into consideration as part of their business calculations. The following statement from one development guide is illustrative:

> As operating costs increase and competition holds prices for goods and services steady, the key to business success continues to be achieving the best profit margin possible. Achieving that maximum profit margin starts from the selection of a competitive business location.... A leading issue today is the availability of workforce development programs. Other issues such as business, sales and income taxes, workers compensation and unemployment legislation and a states's attitude toward business all come in to play (Mooney, 1995).

---

[2] The estimates presented for Figure 6.6 are taken from Brace (1997) and Bartlett and Steele (1998).

Figure 6.6: The Escalating Costs of Jobs to the States

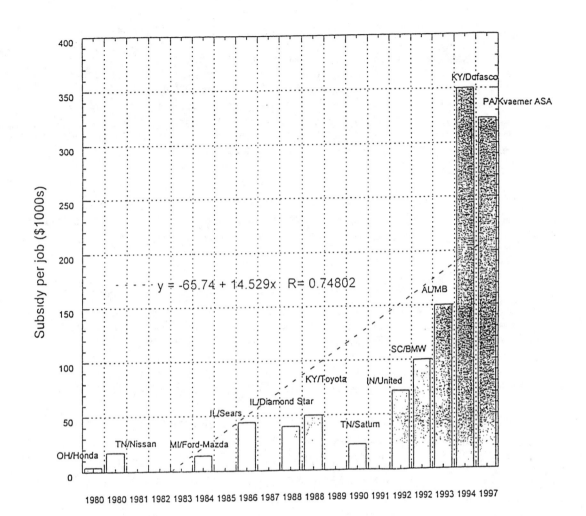

In fact, entire networks of relocation organizations have arisen, offering firms an abundance of information about the best packages and most pliable communities. Days after incorporating a business in Orange County, California, one businessman received a "condolence" card from economic development officials in Nevada listing all the reasons he should have considered locating there (Freidman, 1996). Magazines and journals advise firms on how to exploit state and community largesse and advertise firms with specialties in brokering relocation deals.

A recent account describes what an aspiring entrepreneur can expect to find while searching the Internet today:

> He lands at random on the Indiana Department of Commerce home page, and clicks on the icon labeled "Assistance and Business Incentives." There he finds over twenty different kinds of financial assistance on offer -- from the Capital Access Program and the Hoosier Development Fund to the Indiana Community Business Credit Corporation -- along with export-assistance programs, technical help from the Indiana Micro-Electronics Center and the Indiana Business Modernization and Technology Corporation and seven other programs, and several sorts of workforce assistance... he reflects with gratitude on his country's principled aversion to government meddling in the marketplace, and with even more gratitude on the uneven application of that admirable precept (Donohue, 1997: 75).

While it is probably too early to judge the scope and consequences of the newly emerging economic development networks, initial indications are that the process has been heavily skewed in favor of business and that it typically lacks controls or accountability. One journalistic account describes the extent of this transformation across the country:

> A corporate-welfare bureaucracy of an estimated 11,000 organizations and agencies has grown up, with access to city halls, statehouses, the Capitol and the White House. They conduct seminars, conferences and training sessions. They have their own trade associations. They publish their own journals and newsletters. They create attractive websites on the Internet. And they never call it "welfare." They call it "economic incentives" or "empowerment zones" or "enterprise zones" (Bartlett and Steele, 1998).

In many ways, the most recent wave of economic development is a return to the older forms of firm-chasing, now done with more sophisticated communications and information technology. Far from supplanting old style economic development approaches, the "demand-side" strategies that emerged in the 1980s now appear to serve as mere frosting on already lavish incentive packages available from many states. At the end of the 1990s, the business calculations of many firms may expressly incorporate generous programs from states that will alleviate tax and other burdens, making them more profitable. In fact, to be competitive, many firms may almost be obliged to factor location incentives into their ledgers. If competing firms can reduce prices by extracting large subsides from states or communities, it behooves other firms to follow suit. We must ask to what ends these patterns may take the contemporary states.

FROM WELFARE REFORM TO CORPORATE WELFARE: THE LATEST FACET OF THE NEW POLITICAL ECONOMY

A better appreciation of what states are doing in the area of economic development may be obtained when contrasted with what they are doing less of in the area of welfare. States have retreated from redistributive policy in a manner entirely consistent with

Peterson's expectations. Subnational governments are, according to Peterson (1981 & 1995), ill-suited to pursuing redistributive goals. Donahue (1997: 165) speaks of "state-based policy's built in bias toward undue harshness."

One of the most enthusiastically embraced agenda items in most states under the new federalism has been welfare reform. Cash benefits fell by 42 percent between 1970 and 1993 (Peterson, 1995). In the interest of balanced budgets and low taxes, states have embraced welfare reform almost universally by retreating from playing a role in addressing poverty. Recently, many state leaders supported a welfare reform program that would consolidate all the funds that had been spent on social programs -- such as Aid to Families with Dependent Children (AFDC), Medicaid, and Food Stamps -- and distribute them as massive block grants to the states who would then determine how best to serve the needs of those currently receiving support. Governor Zell Miller of Georgia summarizes how some perceive this change: "I want more flexibility, I want to run these programs without federal strings" (Pear, 1995). For others, however, devolution is a means for cutting back on the welfare state by terminating support programs.

As many states have rushed to reform and often reduce their public assistance efforts, upward redistribution to corporations has grown at an alarming rate. The influence of coalitions promoting public assistance for the needy has declined as the federal role has diminished. In this void, a new constellation of organizations and growing networks has emerged to promote and exploit subsidies for corporations. Today, many states and localities appear much better suited, and much more willing, to address the needs of well-organized and focused corporations than they are of dealing with the poor or working poor.

One might argue that by helping corporations, states and communities may ultimately be helping the needy. In all honesty, it may be too early to tell if these subsidies work, at least in the long-run. The consensus for some time, however, has been that too much is given up in revenues, and too little is gained in jobs, for these packages to produce significant benefits for a state. Many critics of contemporary subsidy packages see them as little more than welfare for corporations. With the paucity of evidence supporting their efficacy, it seems increasingly difficult to justify these subsidy packages as bestowing long-term benefits on the general citizenry and easier to see them as rather brazen grabs for public resources by well-organized interests.

The emergent "demand-side" or "third wave" policies of the 1980s sought to bridge government, universities and business in self-conscious efforts to address economic weaknesses and opportunities in states (Eisinger, 1988; Fosler, 1988). In many contemporary economic development efforts, in contrast, there is an increasing "adhocracy." Many packages aim at specific firms with specific benefits designed to outbid competing jurisdictions with seemingly little attention to the long-term costs of these packages. The interests served by these *ad hoc* efforts, furthermore, seem to be quite narrow.

State-bidding has not gone unnoticed or un-criticized, however. Governor Jim Folsom of Alabama faced a political backlash for courting capital with too little discretion (Donahue, 1997). In 1996, over 100 prominent scholars and policy practitioners in eight Midwestern states signed a petition calling for an end to the economic war among the states (Peirce, 1995). This was reminiscent of an earlier call by the National Governors Association to end predatory competition for employers between states. The popular press has also begun to examine these packages in an increasingly negative manner. At present, however, the structure of largely unregulated lateral competition among states persistently seems to induce policy choices that neither practice nor research has shown to be fruitful.

WHY BAD ECONOMIC DEVELOPMENT STRATEGIES PERSIST

While he takes a nuanced view, Peterson (1995: 188) tends to expect a rational functional sorting pattern to emerge from the ongoing federal devolution. In the emergent functional federalism that Peterson envisions, states are best suited to pursue economic development because they are much more attuned to market signals than the federal government. State and local governments have more direct ways of gauging the effects of their policies. He also reasons that bad policies will not be copied and good policies will be mimicked.

If states were in fact highly responsive to the economic consequences of their policies and if bad policies were not likely to be maintained or mimicked by other states, there would be little cause for concern about the directions economic development seems to be taking at the end of the 1990s. In point of fact, many examples exist of states and communities pursuing ill-fated economic policies, and many other states mimicking them. The questions remains: Why?

It has always been difficult to evaluate the effects of state or local development policies (Eisinger, 1988). National and international economic trends can distort or hide the effects of state level policies (Brace, 1993). The consequences of state tax policies are exceedingly difficult to pin down (Brace, 1994). In the end, many choices seem driven more by political rather than economic contingencies (Brace, 1994). Initial research of electoral outcomes suggested that professionalization in the states had reduced economic accountability among state legislators and governors (Chubb, 1988), that governors were not functionally responsible for the economic health of their states (Stein, 1990), and that there was no discernable relationship between a state's unemployment and inflation rates and voting outcomes for governors (Kenny, 1983). More recent studies of voting behavior provide consistent evidence that voters assign economic accountability to governors (Atkeson and Partin, 1995; Carsey and Wright, 1998; Partin, 1995). The effects of unemployment on governor approval have been shown to be negative and growing over time (Hansen, 1999). It seems quite clear that while it may be difficult to assign rewards for a good economy, state politicians have reason to fear that they will be assigned blame for a bad economy no matter what the source.

Tremendous uncertainty remains about what works and what doesn't; and it is far from clear that states will refrain from policies that are economically disadvantageous in the long-run. When it comes to economic development, the states are in many ways trapped in a classic prisoners' dilemma (Brace, 1993). Collectively, they would be better off if they resisted temptations to engage in predatory competition over jobs. Yet, it is very hard, if not impossible, to enforce collective agreements among the states; and one or several states will almost certainly find it to their advantage to capitalize on opportunities left open when other states practice restraint. These opportunities allow them to deliver highly visible, symbolic, and seeming tangible economic development outcomes in the form of new plants and employers. Given these incentives and the attributes of the economic development policy options available to state policymakers, it is perhaps not too difficult to understand why the choices they make persist despite evidence working against them. These alternative policies embody different beliefs about cause and effect, offer vastly different temporal perspectives about their consequences, and are, thus, likely to elicit very different effects among state constituencies.

Douglas Arnold (1990) provides a provocative and insightful discussion of policy attributes that is particularly useful here. Some policies are single-stage and produce immediate results. Other policies require multiple stages and produce results with either early-order or later-order effects. The longer the causal chain, the more difficult it is for constituents to perform retrospective evaluations and make judgments about the policies. Arnold divides the world into experts, generalists and ordinary citizens, with experts those who evaluate causal chains as part of their jobs, while generalists are the politicians, policy practitioners and commentators who make the actual policy. Ordinary citizens form their opinions somewhat haphazardly about the nature of cause and effect operating in policy areas, but their preferences depend on the incidence of costs and benefits associated with a policy and their beliefs about cause and effect.

In the case of economic development strategies in the states, the old approach is either single stage or short-term in its causal sequence. A package is developed and an offer is made. The incidence of benefits seems clear in the construction of new facilities and the creation of new jobs, while the incidence of costs is quite remote, spread out over many years in the form of industrial bonds, tax abatements and subsidies. The new approach to economic development, which requires investment in technology, training and infrastructure, is clearly multi-stage with a long causal sequence:

Build better schools >>> Have a better workforce >>> Become more productive >>> Get more jobs.

While the benefits are temporally quite remote, the incidence of costs for these complex programs can be quite immediate, especially when they compete with other projects for state tax dollars.

In the late 1980s when state coffers were full from the belt-tightening and tax increases necessitated by the recession a few years before, it seemed entirely plausible that experts were guiding many of the new wave economic policies, while the generalists and ordinary citizens basked in the expansionary economy. The recession of the early 1990s, however, quickly shook the confidence of the general public and many politicians in the utility of these long-range new wave approaches to economic development. Significant backsliding resulted, with the public and politicians in many venues reverting to old forms of competition through subsidy. It seems likely that so long as state politicians are blamed for economic ills, and so long as competition for firms offers voters a seemingly simple solution to complex problems, that this form of economic development activity will persist. The political incentives of the economic development policy options, interacting within the competitive milieu of the evolving federalism, should make it difficult for policymakers and voters to resist short-term approaches. It is a case where democratic processes, combined with political and economic vicissitudes, may produce suboptimal outcomes.

REFERENCES

Anton, T.J. 1984. "Intergovernmental Change in the United States: An Assessment of the Literature," in T.C. Miller, Ed., *Public Sector Performance: A Conceptual Turning Point*. Baltimore: Johns Hopkins University Press.

Arnold, R.D. 1990. *The Logic of Congressional Action*. New Haven: Yale University Press.

Atkeson, L.R. and R.W. Partin. 1995. "Economic and Referendum Voting: A Comparison of Gubernatorial and Senatorial Elections." *American Political Science Review* 89: 99-107.

Bartik, T.J. 1994. "Jobs, Productivity, and Local Economic Development: What Implications Does Economic Research Have for the Role of Government?" *National Tax Journal* 47: 847-861.

Bartlett, D.L. and J.B. Steele. 1998. "Special Report: Corporate Welfare." *Time Magazine*. November 9: 36-49.

Brace, P. 1993. *State Government and Economic Performance*. Baltimore: Johns Hopkins University Press.

Brace, P. 1994. "Choice and Consequence: The Politics and Economics of Tax Change in the American States 1964-1989." Paper presented at the Annual Meeting of the American Political Science Association, New York.

Brace, P. 1997. "Taxes and Economic Development in the American States: Persistent Issues and Notes for a Model," pp. 140-161 in R.D. Bingham and R. Mier, Eds., *Dilemmas of Urban Economic Development: Urban Affairs Annual Review*. Thousand Oaks, CA: Sage.

Brace, P. and D. Ward. 1999. "The Institutionalized Legislature and the Rise of the Anti-politics Era," pp. 71-96 in R. Weber and P. Brace, Eds. *Change and Continuity in American State and Local Government*. Chatham, NJ: Chatham House.

Burstein, M.L. and A.J. Rolnick. 1995. "Congress Should End the Economic War Among the States," pp. 11-17 in *Federal Reserve Bank of Minnesota 1994 Annual Report*. Minneapolis: Federal Reserve Bank of Minnesota.

Carsey, T.M. and G.C. Wright. 1998. "State and National Factors in Gubernatorial Elections." *American Journal of Political Science* 92: 994-1002.

Chubb, J.E. 1988. "Institutions, The Economy and the Dynamics of State Elections." *American Political Science Review* 82: 133-154.

Citizens Research Council of Michigan. 1986. "Municipal Government Economic Development Incentive Programs in Michigan." *Citizens Research Council of Michigan Report No. 280*. Detroit: Citizens Research Council of Michigan.

Donahue, J.D. 1997. *Disunited States*. New York: Basic Books.

Eisinger, P. 1988. *The Rise of the Entrepreneurial State*. Madison: University of Wisconsin Press.

Fosler, R.S. Ed. 1988. *The New Economic Role of the American States*. New York: Oxford University Press.

Freidman, D. 1996. "The New Civil War," pp. 14-31 in *The State of Small Business*. New York: The Goldhirsch Group.

Hansen, S. 1999. "Life is Not Fair: Governors' Job Performance Ratings and State Economies." *Political Research Quarterly* 52: 167-188.

Kenny, P. 1983. "The Effect of State Economic Conditions on the Vote for Governor." *Social Science Quarterly* 64: 154-162.

Mooney, J. 1995. *Doing the Deal: A Developer's Guide to Effective Incentive Utilization*. Plainfield, IN: Indiana Development Services.

Nathan, R.P. and F.C. Doolittle. 1987. *Reagan and the States*. Princeton: Princeton University Press

Osborne, D. 1988. *Laboratories of Democracy*. Boston: Harvard University Business Press.

Partin, R.W. 1995. "Economic Conditions and Gubernatorial Elections: Is the State Executive Held Accountable?" *American Politics Quarterly* 23: 81-95.

Pear, R. 1995. "Governors Helping to Set National Agenda Like Never Before," *New York Times*, January 30, p. A-14.

Peirce, N. 1995. "A Call to End the War Among the States," *Cleveland Plain Dealer*, November 5, p. 9.

Peterson, P. 1981. *City Limits*. Chicago: University of Chicago Press.

Peterson, P. 1995. *The Price of Federalism*. Washington, D.C.: The Brookings Institute.

Regan, E.V. 1988. *Government, Inc.: Creating Accountability for Economic Development Programs*. Chicago: Government Finance Officers Association.

Sabato, L. 1983. *Goodbye to Good-time Charlie*, 2nd Ed. Washington, D.C.: Congressional Quarterly.

Schweke, W., C. Rose, and B. Damson. 1994. *Bidding for Business: Are Cities and States Selling Themselves Short?* Washington, D.C.: Corporation for Enterprise Development.

Stein, R.M. 1990. *Urban Alternatives: Public and Private Markets in the Provision of Local Services*. Pittsburgh: University of Pittsburgh Press.

Van Horn, C. Ed. 1989. *The State of the States*. 2nd Ed. Washington, D.C.: Congressional Quarterly.

Chapter 7

MOVING INTO GLOBAL COMPETITION: A CASE STUDY OF ALABAMA'S RECRUITMENT OF MERCEDES-BENZ

Douglas J. Watson, Edwin I. Gardner, Jr. and Robert S. Montjoy

Globalization is changing the nature of economic development policy in Alabama and in the South more generally. For generations a substantial consensus directed economic development efforts in many Southern states. Beginning with Mississippi's Balance Agriculture with Industry program in the mid-1930's, Southern states developed a strategy based upon enticing industry to relocate there. The lures included cheap land, cheap labor, low taxes, and special incentives in the form of tax breaks and loans. The strategy was successful in bringing a considerable number of manufacturing jobs into the region, but its reliance on a relatively unskilled labor force made the region vulnerable to competition from much cheaper labor as international barriers to trade and capital mobility fell (Cobb, 1993). Some states, such as Florida, consciously adopted a new strategy based upon increased productivity rather than low costs (*Cornerstone*, 1989). In Alabama, a number of economic developers recognized that the old strategy was doomed, but no consensus has developed on a new strategy to take its place.

Ideally, a new strategy would proceed from an informed discussion among policy makers and at least passive acceptance by the public. Often times, however, events become catalysts for decisions which lead to policy debates. Given the accepted need for secrecy in the competitive process of industry recruiting, the public accords its representatives substantial discretion to negotiate deals in the public interest. Yet, departures from the norm will eventually work their way onto the public agenda for at least two reasons. First, the political salience of economic development generally pressures candidates for state office to offer their own programs and to attack those of opponents. Second, a substantial investment of public funds inevitably raises questions about the wisdom of their use.

This chapter provides a case study of Mercedes-Benz's investment in Alabama as an illustration of the dilemma facing Southern economic development officials in the face of globalization's making their traditional strategy obsolete. The recruitment of Mercedes-Benz to Alabama has been widely discussed as an extreme example of the cut-throat competition among the American states that has been dubbed "The New Civil War" (Watson, 1995). Clearly, the bidding for Mercedes was intense, particularly among Southern states; and Alabama paid a very high price by traditional standards. While many criticized the state's incentives as too high a cost for the jobs obtained, some saw Mercedes as an opportunity to effect a necessary change in state development strategy. The manner in which the issues were presented to the public reflected some inherent characteristics of economic development -- high political stakes coupled with the need for secrecy in negotiations. This study examines the way in which the Mercedes recruitment played in the public arena and ultimately influenced a gubernatorial race and offers insights into the process of change in response to economic globalization.

THE BIG PRIZE

In 1993 Daimler-Benz announced that it planned to build its first American automobile manufacturing plant, bringing an estimated 1,400 jobs and a $300 million investment to the site where it would locate. Alabama entered the competition for a variety of reasons. Some developers viewed it as a new level, a Super Bowl, for the traditional game of enticing industry. Some clearly saw the political benefit from landing such a plum. Still others, like Neal Wade, President of the privately funded Economic Development Partnership of Alabama (EDPA), saw it as a chance to move their state into a new game by overcoming the image of backwardness and proving that a quality industry could succeed there. While the incentives offered looked like a continuation of past practices, the jobs would not rely on low-skilled or inexpensive labor. Indeed, the substantial investment that the state would make in training represented an essential step in building the quality workforce that would be needed if Alabama were to upgrade its industrial base.

On the surface the state appeared to endorse the effort. Governor Jim Folsom, Jr. called a special session of the legislature to adopt a new incentive package. The centerpiece was a new tax-break law modeled after Kentucky legislation that had created the Kentucky Rural Economic Development Authority (KREDA) four years earlier. It allowed a company to use the money that it would normally pay to the state in corporate income taxes for debt service on its manufacturing facility. Furthermore, the company could withhold 5 percent of the wages and salaries of its employees and use it for debt service as well. The state, in turn, would then deduct the amount taken from the employees by the company from the amount owed the state in income taxes. Support in the legislature was almost unanimous. Local and private organizations joined in to offer a total incentive package valued at over $300 million.

When Mercedes announced that it would locate near Tuscaloosa, Alabama, the immediate reaction of the announcement was one of pride and jubilation within the state:

Alabama officials were giddy over the announcement, which paired a luxury car company with one of the nation's poorest states, a place known more for racial unrest and football than for stylish, global industry. "This, my friends, is a new day for Alabama, a day when we move to the forefront of economic development," said Gov. Jim Folsom (Reeves, 1993a).

A giant $75,000 Mercedes logo was installed by anonymous corporate donors at Legion Field in Birmingham in time for a nationally televised University of Alabama football game (Jacobson, 1993). EDPA placed full-page advertisements in the *Wall Street Journal*, London's *Financial Times*, and Frankfurt's *Handelsblatt* and announced that it was changing its $1.8 million annual marketing strategy to capitalize on the Mercedes location story (Hansen, 1993).

A number of critics, including many representatives of states that lost the bid, argued that Alabama had paid too much and that the incentive wars among the states were completely out of hand. Yet, a case can be made that Alabama stepped up to a new level with a bold decision. The economic consequences of that decision are still being played out. Certainly, a number of suppliers followed Mercedes to the area, and recently Honda announced the construction of a major facility in Alabama. Criticisms of the price tag might have been short-lived if the strategy had been widely understood and the price had been fully known.

FROM VICTORY TO PUBLIC RELATIONS NIGHTMARE

Certainly, the huge incentives that were offered to Mercedes were anything but noncontroversial. The package was valued at $253.3 million by the Alabama Development Office, the agency primarily responsible for recruiting the company to the state. The state and several local governments committed to infrastructure improvements valued at $77.5 million. They included such projects as water, gas, and sewer line extensions to the site; electrical system improvements; and new roads, including a new interchange on the interstate highway near the site. The state and local governments also offered $92 million of incentives for site development, including purchase and development of the site, at a cost of $30 million; a rail extension; and the construction of a training college/center valued at $30 million.

Several city and county governments participated with the state in offering commitments to the company if it located in Alabama. For example, the Associated Press (1993a) reported the action of the City Council of Tuscaloosa on the Mercedes incentive package:

> The Tuscaloosa City Council upped the ante $30 million Tuesday in the high-stakes bidding war for a Mercedes-Benz plant. The City Council voted unanimously to spend up to $30 million to buy and develop a 1,000 acre site near Vance, 19 miles east of Tuscaloosa. The resolution approved by the City Council provides that the Tuscaloosa County Industrial Development Authority would sell the site to Mercedes-Benz for $100.

Other incentives included waiving sales and use taxes on equipment and material purchased during construction of the facility, as well as on the machinery and equipment bought to be used in the manufacturing process. Through the Economic Development Partnership, an organization funded by thirty-three corporations to promote Alabama, the private sector also committed $15 million to the incentive package.

The critical provisions of the Alabama law that was passed to entice Mercedes were based on the Kentucky KREDA legislation. The company could use the money that it would normally pay to the state in corporate income taxes for debt service on its manufacturing facility. Furthermore, the company could withhold 5 percent of the wages and salaries of its employees and use it for debt service as well. The state, in turn, would then deduct the amount taken from the employees by the company from the amount owed the state in income taxes. The Associated Press (1993d) stated: "That would be the equivalent of letting a person deduct all monthly home payments -- principal and interest -- from personal state income tax as an incentive to move to the state." In essence, then, the state and local governments were paying for the total capital cost of the auto maker building a plant in the United States. The *Wall Street Journal* commented on Alabama's incentive package:

> But what has really stunned economic development experts throughout the South is a package of tax breaks, valued at more than $300 million, that would, among other things, allow Mercedes to pay off its plant with the money it would have spent on state income taxes. "Apparently those people are buying and paying for the whole building," says J. Mac Holladay, who has directed economic development efforts of South Carolina and Mississippi, and was involved in Georgia's bid for the plant. "This steps over the line for the South" (Cooper and Ruffenach, 1993).

Some of the early euphoria in the state over the Mercedes announcement began to fade, furthermore, after the director of the Alabama Development Office (ADO) urged city, county, and educational institutions in the state to buy or lease Mercedes automobiles because "we need to express our support to this company, our gratitude, our appreciation" (Jacobson, 1993). The governor and the ADO director began immediately driving "loaner cars" from Mercedes. The *Birmingham News* editorialized:

> We can appreciate everybody's enthusiasm about the legendary but struggling German automaker deciding to build its new sport vehicle in Alabama.... But this is pandering. This is groveling. This is downright pathetic. This is why people make fun of Alabama. Is our state such an unlikable place that we have to continue buying the good will of Mercedes-Benz? And isn't all this Mercedes over kill an insult to every company that was creating jobs and economic growth in Alabama before the German automaker came along (Jacobson, 1993)?

Furthermore, within days it was revealed that the Alabama recruiting team had committed to purchasing 2,500 of the new sport utility vehicles from Mercedes over a ten-year period as part of the incentive package. The ADO director's recommendation that state agencies, local governments, and educational institutions purchase Mercedes sports utility vehicles was in response to the commitment made by the state in its incentive package to Mercedes.

The value of the commitment to purchase the 2,500 sport vehicles was placed at $75 million and was not included in the analysis released to the public of the costs and benefits to the state of the bid to attract Mercedes. The governor faced an additional problem in making good on his commitment to Mercedes -- a state law passed in 1976 requires state and local agencies to purchase vehicles exclusively from authorized General Motors, Ford, Chrysler, and American Motors dealers. When pressed about this aspect of the incentive package, the governor stated that the whole deal depended on the state's commitment to buy the 2,500 vehicles (Pace, 1993). The governor's decision to offer to purchase the 2,500 vehicles was based on "very reliable information" that South Carolina and North Carolina had agreed to purchase 2,000 of the vehicles from Mercedes as part of their commitment packages. A spokesman for South Carolina's governor denied that their recruiting team had made any offer to purchase vehicles, and North Carolina officials stated their commitment was to buy 1,000 vehicles in one year, not the 2,000 Alabama's governor thought (Pace, 1993).

To complicate matters further, a Birmingham lawyer filed suit in state court to block the purchase by the state or any of its entities. The lawyer argued that the commitment violated state purchasing laws and should be declared illegal and therefore nonbinding. When the case got to court, the lawyers for the state said the commitment was simply "puff" designed to lure Mercedes to Alabama. The *Birmingham News* reported: "[L]awyers for the state said in a court hearing Friday that Alabama officials never intended to buy anything without going through bid laws" (DeMonia, 1994).

The next embarrassing revelation for the governor and the state came only days later. The media revealed that the attorney for the State Revenue Department issued an opinion that the state would be responsible for paying refunds to workers who had too much income tax withheld by their employers from their paychecks under the new industrial incentives law (Reeves, 1993b). Since the actual percentage of tax paid by a worker depends on several factors, such as marital status and the number of dependents, the amount of refunds owed by the state to workers who have had the company withhold the 5 percent "job development fee" was unknown. The Alabama Development Office estimated earlier the total annual benefit to Mercedes for the 5 percent withholding was approximately $42.6 million.

Of course, the new law did not apply to Mercedes exclusively but to any company that met the minimum criteria of creating fifty new jobs, investing $5 million, and paying an average wage of $8 an hour. Companies undertaking expansions in Alabama had only to create twenty new jobs and invest $2 million to take advantage of the incentives legislation (Associated Press, 1994). These modest requirements brought "a number of companies" to apply for the tax breaks, including several that had already committed to building or expanding in Alabama. For example, Hanna Steel Corporation had earlier announced a $30 million expansion in Tuscaloosa before Mercedes had made public its choice of Alabama (Associated Press, 1993c). Hanna made its intentions known to the state that it was planning to fund its expansion utilizing the provisions for the new law.

The public relations problems continued for the governor when the Associated Press broke the following story a few days later:

A black Mercedes-Benz with an $82,000 sticker price is waiting on Gov. Jim Folsom, Jr. at a Montgomery dealership while his staff figures out how to keep taxpayers from getting stuck with the bill. As part of the negotiations to land the Mercedes assembly plant in Tuscaloosa County, Gov. Folsom agreed to use one of the company's luxury sedans as his official state car. Mercedes officials sent a black S420 model to their Montgomery dealer (Associated Press, 1993b).

The governor's legal adviser informed the governor that he could not purchase the automobile with state funds since that action would violate the purchasing law that required competitive bids on any item over $5,000. The governor's staff reportedly sought a company or individual to lease the vehicle from Mercedes and "then re-lease it to the state for use by the governor's office, possibly for $1 per year" (Milazzo, 1993).

A state legislator requested an opinion from the State Ethics Commission on the propriety of the governor asking for corporate or individual contributions to lease the sedan for his use. He wrote: "It would seem if the governor were really concerned about the image of Alabama, he would not beg private business for money so that he could sit behind the wheel of a Mercedes-Benz" (Milazzo, 1993). The Ethics Commission executive director informed the governor's office that it was permissible for an individual or company to lease the vehicle if "the company providing the car should not do business with the state or have dealings with Mercedes-Benz and the car should not be used for political functions" (Staff, 1993). Several months later, the governor's press secretary announced that the governor would not use the Mercedes as his official vehicle because he already had a leased Lincoln at his disposal. She said the governor's promise to use a Mercedes as his official car was simply a "goodwill gesture" and was not binding (DeMonia, 1994).

Another of the Alabama recruiting team's commitments to Mercedes caused more than a minor reaction when it was revealed that the highway from Birmingham to Tuscaloosa was to be renamed the Mercedes Highway. The location of the plant is in the small town of Vance, midway between Birmingham and Tuscaloosa. A state legislator, who was an ardent University of Alabama football fan, proposed that the highway be named after the late football coach Paul "Bear" Bryant and announced that he was planning to introduce a bill in the legislature to have the highway named after the coach. He asked Alabama fans across the state to contact their legislators to support his bill.

A further revelation for Alabama citizens came in a front-page article in the *Wall Street Journal*:

Then came a bombshell. At a late-night meeting... a Mercedes official turned to ask the North Carolina Secretary of Commerce a question. Would the state pick up the salaries of its 1,500 workers for their first year or so on the job, at a cost of $45 million? The workers would be in their training then, and wouldn't be producing anything, Mercedes explained. "I was sitting next to the governor," Mr. Phillips recalls. "We were both shocked. We just said no, right out. I mean, training is one thing, but paying someone's wages?" Alabama, meanwhile, was getting similar questions, and was saying yes, yes, yes, even to the salary request (Browning and Cooper, 1993; see also Hare, 1993).

The Alabama media acknowledged that the governor and his staff had disclosed this commitment at the time of the announcement. However, it was not clearly spelled out that the state would pay the first year or so salaries and wages of the Mercedes workforce. Rather, the commitment was included under a section in the news release concerning training costs. It read that the state would pay "wages, insurance coverages (as determined by MB), allowances and *per diems* for employees during the training period" (Browning and Cooper, 1993). Reporters and other observers did not realize that the training period would include at least the first year of employment for the 1,500 new workers.

Problems for the governor and his industrial recruitment team continued in late December when State Representative Alvin Holmes, a leader of the Legislative Black Caucus, announced that he was planning to file a bill to revoke the incentives bill used to attract Mercedes if the German auto maker did not agree to a set-aside of 30 percent of the jobs and contracts at the manufacturing facility for Blacks (Merelman, 1993). Reportedly, he was angry because an earlier meeting with Mercedes officials was postponed when the head of the project for Mercedes broke his arm in an accident. Holmes seemed to want to antagonize Mercedes as he explicitly charged that "the German people and the German nation have a long history of racism" (Merelman, 1993).

In mid-January, a meeting between Mercedes officials and the state's Black legislators took place in Montgomery. Representative Holmes was apparently satisfied after the meeting, even though the headline in the paper the next day read "Mercedes Makes No Promises" (Merelman, 1994). Holmes reported to the press after the closed-door meeting that Mercedes was committed to fairness: "All individuals regardless of race and color will be treated equally" (Merelman, 1994). The Mercedes spokesman announced that the company would establish a minority advisory board with a goal of strengthening ties with minorities in the state. While Holmes did not agree to withdraw his bills to repeal the incentives law, he told the press he would not "push the bills" (Merelman, 1994).

In late January more controversy broke out when the media reported that the governor had assigned the National Guard to clear the land and prepare the construction site for Mercedes in Vance. Thirty National Guardsmen with numerous pieces of state-owned heavy equipment worked on the 1,000 acre site to shape it so that it would drain properly and allow for the building of the Mercedes plant. The Guardsmen were paid their regular active-duty wages by the state while working at the Mercedes site. The governor defended the use of the National Guard on the grounds that it was good training for the soldiers (Rynecki, 1994).

Critics were quick to question the use of soldiers to prepare the site. One state senator claimed, "I think it's another misuse of government funds. I'm totally shocked. I think we've given Mercedes-Benz enough." Another state senator said: "I have in the past tried to get National Guardsmen to work at schools and they say they can't because they would be in competition with private business. Why can't those National Guardsmen go into some of these poor districts and build an auditorium?" (Rynecki, 1994). Trade organizations were also angry that private construction companies were not able to bid for this large job (Rynecki, 1994). Within days of the media criticism of the National Guard preparing the site for the Mercedes plant, the head of the Guard removed the soldiers. By the end of the month, the Tuscaloosa County Industrial Development Authority announced that it was awarding an $8 million contract to a local construction company to do the necessary site work (Rynecki, 1994).

REVISING THE DEAL

In the Alabama gubernatorial election of 1994, the Mercedes incentive package negotiated by Governor Jim Folsom became a major issue when his opponent, former Governor Fob James, accused him of giving much more than what was needed to attract Mercedes to Alabama. James brought in former Governor Lamar Alexander of Tennessee to campaign for him using the theme that Tennessee attracted two major automobile plants while he was governor for much less than Alabama paid for Mercedes (Bryant, 1994). Many observers believed that James' victory over Folsom in November 1994 was in part attributable to the extent of the incentives given to Mercedes and the manner in which the matter was handled (Myerson, 1996).

Even before taking office as governor, Fob James announced that one of his first acts would be to propose sweeping changes in the Folsom incentives law to the Alabama legislature. He questioned its legality and felt that it was much too generous. At the time James took office in January 1995, the Alabama Development Office had already approved eighty-six new and expanding industries for the tax breaks allowed under the Folsom incentives law. While opposing the Folsom incentives law publicly, James apparently reassured Mercedes officials that he had no plans to withdraw the State's commitment to that company:

> Asked about keeping the State's $253 million in tax breaks and financial commitments to the Mercedes assembly plant, Mr. James said, "I'm committed to do what it takes to keep the Mercedes project on stream. Now, commitments that are illegal have to be worked upon. Commitments made that are extraordinarily illegal cannot be ignored" (Rawls, 1995a).

The most serious legal threat to the Folsom incentives law and to the particular tax breaks promised to Mercedes was a lawsuit promised by the Alabama Education Association (AEA). The AEA contended that the State Constitution requires all income taxes to be used for education. Since the incentives law permitted the abatement of income taxes, the AEA believed that it was on strong ground to have the law declared illegal. Industrial developers in Alabama felt that the threat of the lawsuit by the AEA was enough to kill the bill. Dara Longgrear, executive director of the Tuscaloosa County Industrial Development Authority, said if the law is in litigation, "what company is going to apply for it?" (Associated Press, 1995). Governor James persuaded the AEA to withhold filing its lawsuit until he could develop a bill for the Legislature that would substantially amend the Folsom incentives law.

While James assured Mercedes officials that the State would keep its commitments to them, he said that the other eighty-six companies that qualified for the same aid under the Folsom act could not be guaranteed that they would receive it. The number of jobs created by the eighty-six companies was estimated at 12,328 and the total investment at more than $3.3 billion. The acting director of the Alabama Development Office said that these companies would be urged to utilize the provisions of the bill that James would propose to the Legislature when it came into session in April 1995 (Sawyer, 1995). By early March 1995, officials of the James Administration would not reveal the details of the proposed bill to be presented to the Legislature the next month.

James faced an immediate problem with the commitments made to Mercedes. Under the agreement between the State and Mercedes, the State agreed to pay Mercedes up to $42.6 million toward the cost of its plant construction as early as April 1, 1994. Governor Folsom had planned to issue bonds to make the payment, but Governor James initially did not want to use that financing vehicle and sought an alternative. Eventually, James proposed a bond issue of $145 million to pay the Mercedes commitments using the Alabama Trust Fund, a gas and oil trust fund that generates approximately $60 million annually for the State, as the revenue source to make the debt service payments.

However, after the State Legislature passed James' bill to issue the bonds for Mercedes, the Alabama Supreme Court ruled that the new law was an unconstitutional diversion of the interest income of the Alabama Trust Fund from the state's General Fund (Rawls, 1995b). James then proposed a tax on credit cards that are issued by out-of-state banks, but strong opposition from the Alabama Bankers Association killed this gambit. Out of desperation, Governor James turned to the Retirement Systems of Alabama (RSA) for a loan of $140 million to pay the Mercedes commitments. The State is forbidden by its Constitution from borrowing so the money from the RSA was labeled as a "shift among state agencies." David Bronner, the head of the RSA, set the interest rate for the loan at nine percent (2.5 percent above the market rate at the time), which he described as a "punitive rate." The Legislature quickly considered and enacted a bill to repay the loan to the RSA (Poovey, 1995).

On May 4, 1995, Governor James' plan to revise the Alabama incentives law was introduced in the State Legislature. The proposal sharply curtailed the generous incentives of the existing bill and placed a cap on the amount of benefits that a company could receive using the corporate income tax. Importantly, the bill also "grandfathered" all existing incentive agreements with companies that took advantage of the Folsom incentives act (Rountree, 1995). Eventually, Governor James satisfied Mercedes officials that the state would keep the promises made to it by the Folsom Administration. The Governor did renegotiate some of the promises, such as the state's commitment to purchase 2,500 sport utility vehicles manufactured at the Alabama plant. Since state law prohibits the purchase of automobiles from other than American manufacturers, Mercedes accepted the Governor's refusal to purchase the vehicles.

ALABAMA ENTERS A "NEW GAME"

Globalization is changing the nature of economic development in Alabama. It is forcing the state to abandon its traditional strategy based upon low production costs, but it also created an opportunity for Alabama to recruit a renowned international company and to begin selling itself on the basis of productivity and quality. The processes of making and implementing the decision to lure Mercedes to Alabama were anything but smooth. In fact, the recruitment appears to have been the product of multiple actors with multiple goals and strategies. Certainly, the Governor was eager to take credit for the coup but failed to reveal its full costs or to articulate the strategy that might have justified them in the eyes of the electorate. Piece-meal disclosure tended to discredit later explanations. Yet, despite the problems and the costs, Alabama is now a stronger player in the global game of economic development than it was before. The ML320 has been well received, and Mercedes expanded its production goals to meet demand. A 1999 study showed 9,773 jobs created directly and indirectly by Mercedes and its suppliers. Recently, Honda announced a major facility to be built in the state, and Boeing's decision to build a new rocket plant in Alabama further strengthened the state's claim to a higher rung on the productivity ladder. It appears that the decision to jump-start Alabama's entry into the global market on the basis of quality and productivity, rather than low costs, has been at least initially successful.

Globalization is clearly changing the game of economic development, but the emerging rules and optimal strategies of the new game are not necessarily clear to all of the players in the contest. The Mercedes case illustrates the rough and uncertain nature of transition steps taken in the absence of a consensus on direction. From the perspective of the traditional economic development strategy, the price of the jobs initially promised by Mercedes seemed high; and, certainly, the ultimate cost was increased by the intense competition among the bidding states. Yet from another perspective, the incentives offered by Alabama can be viewed as "table stakes" for the new global game of economic development.

REFERENCES

Associated Press. 1993a. "Council Oks Mercedes Site Funding," *Montgomery Advertiser*, September 22, p. 5B.

Associated Press. 1993b. "$82,000 Mercedes Ready for Folsom," *Montgomery Advertiser*, November 20, p. 1A.

Associated Press. 1993c. "Other Companies Are Already Trying to Use Mercedes Bill," *Opelika-Auburn News*, November 12, p. A2.

Associated Press. 1993d. "State Aims to Lure Mercedes Plant," *Columbus Ledger-Enquirer*, August 6, p. A3.

Associated Press. 1994. "New Guidelines Set for Tax Incentives," *Montgomery Advertiser*, January 21, p. 5B.

Associated Press. 1995. "Teachers Vow Mercedes Law Illegal," *Birmingham News*, March 8, p. A5.

Browning, E.S. and H. Cooper. 1993. "States' Bidding War over Mercedes Plant Made for Costly Chase," *Wall Street Journal*, November 24, p. A6.

Bryant, T. 1994. "Shots Fired Over Mercedes," *Birmingham Post-Herald*, November 2, pp. B1 & B4.

Cobb, J.C. 1993. *The Selling of the South: The Southern Crusade for Industrial Development, 1936-1990*. Urbana: University of Illinois Press.

Cooper, H. and G. Ruffenach. 1993. "Mercedes Expected to Choose Alabama for Plant, But State's Price Will Be Steep," *Wall Street Journal*, September 30, pp. A2 & A12.

Cornerstone: Growing the Future. 1989. Tallahassee: Florida Chamber of Commerce.

DeMonia, R. 1994. "Governor Backs Off Use of Mercedes as Official Car," *Birmingham News*, March 19, p. 10A.

Hansen, J. 1993. "They'll Look Twice at Alabama," *Birmingham News*, October 10, p. 1D.

Hare, K. 1993. "'Free' Enterprise," *Montgomery Advertiser*, November 29, p. 10A.

Jacobson, J.E. 1993. "Camp's Cars," *Birmingham News*, October 25, p. 4A.

Merelman, S. 1993. "Bills Target Mercedes Benefits," *Montgomery Advertiser*, December 28, p. 3B.

Merelman, S. 1994. "Mercedes Makes No Promises," *Montgomery Advertiser*, January 19, p. 3B.

Milazzo, J.D. 1993. "Mercedes Deal Hits Another Bump," *Montgomery Advertiser*, November 23, pp. 1A & 4A.

Myerson, A.R. 1996. "O Governor, Won't You Buy Me a Mercedes Plant?" *New York Times*, September 1.

Pace, D. 1993. "State's Offer Saved Deal, Folsom Says," *Montgomery Advertiser*, November 9, p. 3B.

Poovey, B. 1995. "RSA Loan to Pay Off Benz Debt," *Montgomery Advertiser*, June 22, p. 3B.

Rawls, P. 1995a. "James Aiming to Trim Business Incentives Package," *Montgomery Advertiser*, January 14, p. 3F.

Rawls, P. 1995b. "James Mulling Credit Card Tax to Pay Mercedes," *Montgomery Advertiser*, June 21, p. 3B.

Reeves, J. 1993a. "Alabama Basks in Official Unveiling of Mercedes-Benz Deal," *Columbus Ledger-Enquirer*, October 1, p. A1.

Reeves, J. 1993b. "Tax Law Worth Millions to Mercedes," *Montgomery Advertiser*, November 12, p. 1A.

Rountree, D. 1995. "Incentives Revisions Criticized," *Montgomery Advertiser*, May 5, p. 3B.

Rynecki, D. 1994. "Folsom Calls on Guard of Benz Site," *Birmingham Post-Herald*, January 21, pp. A1 & A3.

Sawyer, S. 1995. "ADO Chief: Counting on Benz Tax Breaks Risky," *Montgomery Advertiser*, February 28, p. 5D.

Staff. 1993. "Ethics Chief Warns Folsom of Using Cars," *Montgomery Advertiser*, November 24, p. 3B.

Watson, D J. 1995. *The New Civil War*. Westport, CT: Praeger.

Chapter 8

CHARLOTTE'S RESPONSE TO GLOBALIZATION: THE MAYOR'S INTERNATIONAL CABINET[1]

Harry I. Chernotsky

The increasing pace of globalization is impacting considerably on numerous cities across the United States. Relatively few have advanced to the point where they might be counted among the elite core of world cities. Yet, more and more are being forced to respond to changes in trade, immigration, and the movement of capital which link them more directly to the global economy. Of particular interest are the new political configurations and collaborations developing to promote local economic development. This paper examines one community -- Charlotte, North Carolina -- where expanding linkages to the world economy have elicited concerted policy response. It focuses on the Mayor's International Cabinet, a rather innovative public-private partnership designed to spearhead the formation and implementation of the city's International Strategic Plan. This review assesses the work of the Cabinet, especially in terms of establishing priorities and generating support for policy initiatives relating to Charlotte's globalization. It also explores the applicability of Charlotte's approach for other newly internationalizing cities.

SOURCES OF EXPANDING GLOBAL-LOCAL CONNECTIONS

The involvement of American cities in the international arena is not a new phenomenon. Indeed, such activities have long been a necessity to promote economic growth and development. Relatively few (New York, Los Angeles and perhaps Chicago) have advanced to the point where they might be counted among the elite core of "world

[1]This work was supported, in part, by funds provided by the University of North Carolina at Charlotte. The author is indebted to Jennifer Watson Roberts for her input and assistance.

cities" which have come to occupy critical positions as control points in the increasingly interdependent global economy (Abu-Lughod, 1995: 176-183). Changes in patterns of communication, transportation, trade, immigration and the movement of capital have prompted expansion in the number and types of modern "city-states" whose fates are linked *directly* to the international system (Peirce, 1993: 5). Many are beginning to respond independently to issues traditionally handled by higher levels of government (Alger, 1988: 322-323).

The imperatives of complex interdependence and the progressive internationalization of production have been particularly important stimuli. As the volume of international trade and investment has expanded, so has the number of U.S. jobs linked directly to the global economy. In 1997, close to thirteen million U.S. jobs were related to the nearly $2 trillion in trade activities, while an additional five million Americans worked for foreign companies whose cumulative U.S. investments had exceeded $700 billion. Most significantly, major metropolitan areas have been the source of approximately three-quarters of U.S. exports and particularly popular sites for foreign businesses (Bach, 1997: 18; *Wall Street Journal*, 1996). Locally supported export assistance programs, incentive packages to lure reverse investment, and enhanced cooperative linkages are a few of the more common strategies emerging to capitalize on the opportunities presented (Fry, 1993: 30-35). Although exerting minimal influence over the direction of broader U.S. foreign policy decisions, municipal governments are becoming more proactive in responding to these developments and are exploring new mechanisms to enhance their capabilities in the pursuit of transnational relations (Cohn, et. al., 1989: 75).

Changing relationships with federal and state governments have also convinced local authorities of the need to seek out new avenues to secure necessary revenues and resources. Federal transfer payments, which accounted for approximately 26 percent of total state and local government expenditures in 1980, have declined to less than 21 percent (*New York Times*, 1996a). Meanwhile, fewer of those funds can be directed toward economic development purposes when they are needed to cover expanding individual entitlements and mandates requiring the provision of welfare and other basic services. Additional pressures have resulted from the reduction of state transfer payments to local governments. Accounting for approximately 34 percent of state expenditures in 1970, these outlays have dropped to around 28 percent (*New York Times*, 1996b). These figures help explain how the pursuit of international opportunities to augment existing funds, add to tax bases, and generate additional employment fits well with both local needs and federal-state interests in reducing urban management obligations in the era of "fend for yourself federalism."

Finally, the increasing professionalization of local governments makes them better equipped to handle a more active international role. Local leaders are being required to react in a more entrepreneurial fashion to a new opportunity structure, even as they often confront a shortage of available public resources with which to do so. This is spurring a rather considerable degree of experimentation involving a restructuring of traditional roles and responsibilities (Clarke, 1993: 11). The privatization of city services and the forging of new partnerships with business, higher education and non-governmental organizations are a few of the more popular techniques being utilized (Harris, 1997:

1699). Meanwhile, the experiences of local governments in the realm of intergovernmental diplomacy are serving to enhance crucial bargaining skills, while the expanding numbers of local organizations and groups with stakes in matters international provide the political impetus to pursue new avenues based upon the "think globally, act locally" idea (Kincaid, 1989: 227). Participation of leaders from both the public and private sectors in overseas missions sponsored by such organizations as the National League of Cities and the U.S. Conference of Mayors has been particularly helpful in this regard.

As more and more U.S. cities find themselves plugged into the foreign relations sphere, they will be cast in a variety of roles in which they may function as:

- partners in foreign policy development through indirect representation in the Congress;
- pressure points in the policy making process by virtue of the increasing salience of "intermestic issues;"
- self governing political communities affecting international ties through their powers of taxation, regulation, service provision and law enforcement;
- promoters of area interests in the global marketplace;
- parties to agreements and compacts with foreign powers for so long as those ties do not intrude on the federal government's prerogatives; and
- practitioners of goodwill through their encouragement and involvement in exchanges and other programs to promote international understanding (Kincaid, 1989: 6-9).

STRATEGIES AND APPROACHES

The cities involved in translating their international interests into concerted activity have adopted wide ranging strategies and techniques. This diversity of approach is endorsed by the National League of Cities, which has encouraged the development of individually-tailored action plans built upon prevailing community strengths (National League of Cities, 1997: 2-6). Given budgetary and other logistical constraints, efforts have often focused on expanding the mandates and responsibilities of existing bodies while tapping into the available resources of engaged community groups and organizations.

As the forces of globalization penetrate deeper into many communities, local leaders find themselves resorting more and more to symbolic or "conscious-raising" measures designed to heighten international sensitivities and awareness (Shuman, 1986/87: 159-160). Broad vision statements have become fairly popular devices used by officials to generate support for economic planning with a distinctively international bent (Harris, 1997: 1700). These may prove useful in building the coalitions necessary to proceed with more concrete measures requiring the expenditure of resources. Promotional efforts on behalf of international education programs, sponsorship of events and festivals celebrating foreign cultures, and support for research specifying the impacts of global forces on the local economy are also among the relatively simple and inexpensive steps that can help transform attitudes and build strategic political support for a more expansive international agenda.

Yet, community leaders also have access to any number of substantive capabilities when seeking to extend these international connections. On occasion, they may even be found flexing their tax, police, zoning, contracting or investing powers unilaterally to influence the direction of national foreign policy (Shuman, 1986/87: 160-161). These may include steps to deprive specific companies or entire countries deemed "guilty" of negative behaviors (e.g., South Africa during the apartheid era and Switzerland due to recent allegations of complicity in support of Nazi Germany) from realizing locally-derived benefits through the sale of products or the securing of contracts. More commonly, unilateral manipulations of this sort are less punitive in nature and directed more toward enhancing local economic development prospects. To this end, efforts tend to focus on crafting environments more conducive to the expansion of trade, investment or tourist opportunities.

Economic interests are also pivotal in the forging of bilateral foreign contacts and accords initiated at the local level (Shuman, 1986/87: 161). This even extends to Sister City agreements, one of the more popular programs promoting local/global connections. By 1996, approximately 1,100 municipalities had connected with 1,770 cities in 122 countries. An estimated 150,000 Americans annually travel to their partner cities as a result of these arrangements, most of which are accompanied by cooperative economic projects (Sister Cities, 1996: 1 & 3). Designed primarily to build cross-cultural understanding, these types of programs are quite useful as conduits in broadening the scope of international involvement. They perform important *expressive* functions by generating the kind of awareness necessary to stimulate concrete action. Often undertaken for specific purposes and to bring about measurable impacts, they also play an *instrumental* role in tapping the economic potential of globalization by providing the impetus and support for institutionalizing such involvements (Hobbs, 1994: 70-71). To fully maximize these opportunities, however, local leaders are turning increasingly to new approaches and arrangements.

Political innovation has become increasingly critical in responding to the demands of globalization. Public officials often find themselves under considerable pressure to react aggressively and creatively to economic opportunities even as they are compelled to address other existing community needs and issues. Their ability to pursue a more entrepreneurial approach may be limited further, moreover, by bureaucratic constraints and the absence of available public resources. The need for greater flexibility and adaptability to tap the local economic development potential of globalization has produced some rather interesting experimentation (Crahan and Vourvoulias-Bush, 1997).

Of particular significance is the horizontal restructuring of private-public sector relationships. This may be seen as part of a "new localism" entailing fundamental changes in the division of authority and responsibility and a reconstituting of local government roles relative to the market (Goetz and Clarke, 1993). Heightened private sector participation in the economic development process creates opportunities for new leadership and fresh approaches that may be applied more quickly. It is also quite helpful in gaining more immediate and direct access to private funds and other resources that might be utilized for broader economic development purposes.

In this environment, city officials may be seen adopting broker roles as facilitators of economic growth and promoters of policy innovation and cooperation. This serves to narrow the distance between the public and private sectors, while fostering the creation of new partnerships and decision frameworks to address the challenges and needs brought about by the advancing forces of globalization. Non-profit organizations and quasi-public agencies have become especially important components of this new policy mix, contributing to the shift in power away from the exclusive preserve of elected bodies and toward those controlling private resources (Clarke, 1993: 12-18; Clarke and Gaile, 1997: 31-34).

Even as the scope and breadth of these sorts of activities have increased, "turf battles" with the federal government have remained limited. Earlier initiatives on behalf of nuclear test bans and freezes, South African divestment, and Central American political refugee sanctuaries generated some controversy but were of limited duration. On occasion, direct forays into the international arena have also evoked local opposition, especially when they seek to influence or alter broader policy objectives through specific actions. Local officials tend to be seen as inexperienced, ill suited to these sorts of policy matters, and even capable of harming national interests when seeking to elevate their own particularistic concerns (Hobbs, 1994: 77-79). This was the case in Seattle, where a City Council resolution declaring the city a sanctuary for Central American refugees was repealed by a voter initiative instructing officials to "avoid diversions of their time and city funds for the consideration or obstruction of foreign policy and immigration matters" (Seattle Municipal Archives, 1985-86).

For the most part, local authorities are careful to stay within the bounds of acceptable behavior (Bilder, 1989: 828). With no real constitutional authority to participate in foreign affairs, they are unlikely to challenge the federal government's monopoly over the tools of foreign policy and appear especially cognizant of the prohibitions against obstruction as they relate to the issues of "high" politics (Shuman, 1986/87: 162). As international economic issues gain additional importance, controversy may arise over the constitutional power accorded the Congress (through the Commerce Clause of Article I) to regulate commercial arrangements. To date, conflict here has been kept to a minimum due to the 1983 Supreme Court ruling that states and local governments are not subject to the restraints of the Commerce Clause when entering the market (Shuman, 1986/87: 166). Future efforts in such areas as trade and investment promotion could prove more troublesome, however, when prevailing national policy is seen as an obstacle to local economic interests. This is suggested by reaction to requirements imposed by the World Trade Organization (WTO), especially as they relate to local powers over product safety, subsidies and labeling (Shuman, 1998: 31-36).

The most serious legal encumbrance encountered thus far has come from the decision of the Supreme Court in the 1968 *Zschernig v. Miller* case. Ruling on an Oregon statute prohibiting resident aliens from inheriting property when reciprocal opportunities are not extended, the Court found the law an unjustified intrusion into the foreign policy powers of the federal government. Yet, in subsequent years, the Court has not sought to expand upon this ruling and has even upheld the right of others to similar intrusions. Thus, despite the rather broad constraints suggested by the language of *Zschernig,* few cities have been deterred by legal considerations in their efforts to assert themselves internationally (Shuman, 1986/87: 166-167).

SOME RECENT INNOVATIONS

The range of cities adopting new modes of operation in pursuing their international interests is rather impressive. The list includes cities with extended and long standing connections abroad, as well as those which might lay claim to "world class" status by virtue of their multi-faceted endowments. Of particular interest are some of the newcomers just beginning to tap the potential of transnational activity, those cities seeking to carve out particular niches in the global marketplace and those whose rather limited international orientation would seem to make them unlikely candidates for such initiatives (Fry, et. al., 1989; Knox, 1997). In these cases, increasing exposure has been critical in spawning the leadership and supporting networks necessary to proceed (Knox, 1997: 21-23).

In Dallas, the findings of the 1987 Mayor's Commission on International Development prompted the creation of the Office of International Affairs (OIA) with a mandate to exploit and expand the broad range of political, economic and cultural activities necessary to promote internationalization. The commitment to this "municipal foreign ministry" operating out of City Hall was reflected in the use of city money to fund its professional and support staff. However, the need to rely exclusively on private funding for its entire operating budget suggested the still somewhat fragile nature of this type of institution building. Even in a community where the international sector was quite visible and where public-private cooperation was extensive, it was difficult to generate financial support for an office seen as somewhat peripheral to traditional government functions (*Clearinghouse*, February-March 1994: 1-2).

The same sorts of financial restraints affected other key cities known for their innovation in this area (Charlotte Economic Development Department, 1992). In San Francisco, for example, the need to generate private funding was critical even as the Office of the Mayor was becoming the focal point for internationalization. The negotiating of Sister City relationships provided some of the initial impetus for looking to international resources to augment the city's economic base. The Mayor's Office of Business and Economic Development was particularly active in this regard, working closely with the private sector in securing overseas contacts, attracting foreign investment, and designing joint projects to promote local growth. The city's diverse population base proved quite helpful in generating local support for these efforts, while its extensive foreign visitor-tourist activity led to the creation of an Office of Protocol financed through private funds to foster a more "user friendly" environment (Fry, 1991: 25-34). It is important to note the continuing importance of the Office of the Mayor in facilitating these activities. Over the past few years, the Mayor has led missions comprised of public and private sector members to Europe and Asia in pursuit of trade, investment and other economic opportunities to promote local development (Fry, 1998: 15-16; Walker, 1996: 82-83).

The key role of the Mayor's office also was noteworthy in Atlanta's emergence as an international city. The process was facilitated by a particularly strong business climate and by the commitment of the private sector to support a comprehensive approach to globalization (Soldatos, 1989: 41-54). The city's efforts to promote a more integrated regional strategy, especially with regard to attracting foreign businesses and international institutions, also proved useful in enhancing its reputation as the "South's capital city" and in laying the groundwork for securing the 1996 Olympic games (Allen, 1996).

In terms of coordination and strategic planning, Seattle presents an especially impressive case. With its extensive foreign commercial ties, tourism, connections to international financial and economic networks, and increasing cultural diversity, Seattle had considerable experience as an international city. Recognizing the need to provide for a more systematic approach in managing these links, a four-person Office of International Affairs (OIA) was established within the city's executive department in 1986. The city's approximately twenty Sister City organizations came under the direction of the OIA, as did a full range of internationally-related activities impacting on economic development. The OIA Director answered directly to the Mayor, who was generally viewed as the chief protocol officer of the region (Charlotte Economic Development Department, 1992: 3). Although subsequently incorporated into the Office of Intergovernmental Relations, the international affairs division continues to enjoy the support of the Mayor and the City Council while performing a series of vital roles in managing and coordinating the international interests of Seattle's city government (Yuthok, 1997).

The Trade Development Alliance of Greater Seattle (TDA) also serves as a model of regional cooperation in pursuit of the benefits of the global economy. This public-private partnership was established in 1991, through the leadership of the Greater Seattle Chamber of Commerce, in recognition of the need for collaboration to retain the region's competitiveness (*Clearinghouse*, August-September 1992: 1-2). Over the years, the size and activities of the TDA have expanded steadily. It is now comprised of six partner organizations, representing key public and private interests across the region. It is governed by an active executive board including elected city and surrounding county officials, labor representatives, the President of the Chamber, and leading members of the region's business and financial communities. Through its work (including the organizing of overseas trade missions, the hosting of inbound international delegations, and the development of marketing strategies), the TDA has assumed a key role in promoting the global economic interests of the region while lending needed coherence to those efforts (Stafford, 1997).

CHARLOTTE AND THE WORLD: THE
MAYOR'S INTERNATIONAL CABINET

With a number of models upon which to draw, a critical mass of people aware of important changes taking place with respect to the international dimension of Charlotte came together in the early 1990's to press for local government action. Several citizens representing the private, education and non-profit sectors approached the Mayor with the idea of seeking greater coordination to tap the economic development potential of globalization. A small International Task Force was appointed, but nothing much was accomplished because the Mayor was nearing the end of her tenure. Generating grass roots support for any significant initiative was a somewhat difficult sell. It was still a bit premature to label Charlotte as one of the "new international cities" emerging across North America even as it was developing as one the country's premiere commercial banking centers (Fry, et. al., 1989). Yet, there was growing evidence of the city's global connections. To begin with, Charlotte was becoming a more diverse community. According to the 1990 census (whose count was generally acknowledged to be low), 17,875 of Mecklenburg County's 507,500 residents were foreign born. When factoring in second and third generation family members, it was estimated that perhaps as many as ten percent of the county's residents could trace their roots to a foreign country ("Charlotte Becomes a Melting Pot," 1993). This reflected a radical change for an area where cultural differences were depicted almost exclusively along a racial divide.

Charlotte's international business links were also expanding rapidly. According to U.S. Department of Commerce figures, the Charlotte metropolitan area was one of the country's fastest growing export markets with manufacturing exports rising 254 percent between 1987 and 1993, far outstripping the national average of 90 percent during that same period. Ranking twenty-fourth among cities in terms of overall export sales, local companies accounted for approximately $1.8 billion of exports in 1993 -- up considerably from the $500 million level in 1987 ("Charlotte Logs Fastest Growth," 1994). This success was attributable, in part, to the assistance of a developing local export infrastructure spearheaded by the Greater Charlotte Chamber of Commerce. It also corresponded to export growth at the state level (21.9 percent in 1994) and North Carolina's rise to tenth place among all states in terms of export value -- $13.7 billion (*Charlotte International Review*, 1995: 15-16).

Also impressive was Charlotte's attraction to foreign companies. By 1994, more than half (122) of the 238 foreign-owned firms with headquarters in North Carolina were located in the area. They represented a range of activities and countries of origin and provided approximately fifteen thousand jobs (KPMG, 1994: 8-16). By 1995, the total number reached 321, with another 150 located within the fifteen surrounding counties comprising the broader Charlotte region (*Charlotte International Review*, 1995: 23 & 34). Their presence contributed to the development of support groups such as the British American Business Round Table and the French American Business Alliance.

At the same time, people moving to the region from abroad and from other large urban areas were beginning to stimulate the growth of local organizations and institutions focused on international themes. International House (a non-profit organization established in 1985 to serve the interests of internationals), the Charlotte World Affairs Council, and the Charlotte World Trade Association were enjoying particular success; global education programs were developing at all levels; Honorary Consuls were operating on behalf of four countries (Britain, France, Germany, Mexico); and the Sister

Cities program was proceeding with an ambitious agenda for expansion (*International Charlotte*, 1994).

These developments were not lost on the new Mayor, who responded favorably to lobbying by a number of community leaders advocating greater coordination and systematic planning to strengthen Charlotte's image as an international city (Josephson, 1992). Within a few months of taking office, he resurrected the International Task Force and went so far as to assign the head of the city's Economic Development Department to direct its efforts. In an effort to gain a better sense of direction and purpose, other cities involved in activities to promote globalization were contacted. The results of this probe were to have profound impacts on Charlotte's future direction.

First, it was clear that economic development was the driving force in the internationalization process and provided the fuel for coordination and planning. This was relevant to Charlotte where the growth in the number of exchange programs, foreign students and language programs, for example, was attributed to businesses in need of workers with the necessary skills to operate in the global economy. Second, the role of the Mayor was seen as especially critical in those cities which were moving to institutionalize their activities (note the previous discussion of Dallas, San Francisco, Atlanta and Seattle). As chief executive, the Mayor's ability to coordinate and direct development from a central location was seen as pivotal. The Mayor was also the person whom foreigners expected to contact and have at official functions, such as the opening of new Sister City relationships and the welcoming of overseas trade missions. Third, these cities had the equivalent of international departments with full time staff dedicated to working with international business, cultural and educational exchanges, and services for international residents (Charlotte Economic Development Department, 1992).

These findings convinced the Mayor to move forward with the process. The International Task Force was renamed the Mayor's International Cabinet to emphasize the intention of the Mayor to assume a lead role in this area and to suggest a sense of permanence. The charge to the members was to "serve as the principal advisors to the Mayor about international affairs so that he can provide effective leadership on behalf of the community." The Cabinet's initial mandate included the development of a Strategic Plan outlining the priorities and actions required to enable the city to confront the challenges and opportunities of globalization (*The Business Journal*, 1992). In addition to providing needed focus, this exercise was intended to capture the attention of those local groups most affected by globalization and those whose support would be critical to the success of the Cabinet's efforts.

Even with a formal structure in place, the Cabinet emerged as a rather informal body. Its charter members were selected partly through expressed interest and partly by trying to capture the key community players in the international game. No additional criteria were seen as necessary at this point. The Cabinet was divided into three main "wings" -- international services and cultural affairs, educational relationships, and economic development -- which were to generate the issues to be addressed in the Strategic Plan. A Visibility Committee was also formed to begin promoting "International Charlotte," while educating the local community about the changing character of the city to build support for future Cabinet projects (*Cabinet Minutes*, June 15, 1992).

Early Cabinet meetings focused on preparing an international vision statement for the city and planning for the development of the Strategic Plan outlining measures necessary to realize this vision. The city's Economic Development chief assumed leadership but had only limited time to devote to the administration of the Cabinet. If the Cabinet was to progress further, a full time staff person was required (Rosenstrauch, 1995). A relatively unknown commodity with few direct ties to the City Council, the Cabinet was in no position to secure additional funding. A stroke of luck may have been the most critical factor in sustaining the Cabinet at this point. The U.S. Department of State had recently established the Pearson Fellowship program, which gave approximately fourteen foreign service officers a year away from their regular duties to share their foreign policy expertise with local communities across the country. Although rejected initially, Charlotte's 1993-94 application resulted in the assigning of a Fellow whose salary would be covered by the State Department if supplemented by a $10,000 city contribution (*Cabinet Minutes*, December 7, 1992). Coincidentally, four months before the Fellow was scheduled to take up her duties as Cabinet administrator, someone with recent foreign service experience moved to Charlotte and agreed to assume the leadership post temporarily in April 1993. With someone in place to coordinate meetings and activities, the Cabinet was now poised to gain momentum and enhance its presence within the community (*Cabinet Minutes*, June 7, 1993).

Even as work on the Strategic Plan was proceeding, questions began arising from within the Cabinet itself as to the priorities, direction and prospective impact of the body. The issue of future funding was of particular concern. Meanwhile, the Cabinet's work was drawing others into the planning process and even spawning new initiatives. International House formed an Advocacy Council which brought together representatives from various groups working with Charlotte's growing international community. A report listing priorities and goals for city services in this area was produced; and many of these were incorporated into the Strategic Plan (*Cabinet Minutes*, December 12, 1994). The Cabinet also was beginning to assume a unique role in the area of economic development. With its exclusive focus on international issues, it gave companies or individuals specifically interested in foreign investment, international trade and other foreign involvement a specialized group with which to share concerns and discuss coordinating activities (*Cabinet Minutes*, June 7, 1993).

Preparing the Strategic Plan took over a year. This was longer than anticipated but helped the Cabinet to maintain its sense of purpose. Anticipating considerable publicity and circulation, members recognized the importance of keeping the plan straightforward, direct, and focused on their "International Vision for the 21st Century" emphasizing Charlotte's intention to develop:

- a citizenry recognizing the importance of the city's international relationships;
- civic and business leaders committed to building an international city; and
- a supportive local environment and the expansion of opportunities and linkages (City of Charlotte, 1994: 2).

In the spring of 1994, the final version of the Plan was adopted formally by the Cabinet (*Cabinet Minutes*, April 25, 1994). This was an especially important milestone in the development of the body. Unveiled by the Mayor at a July press conference, the Plan identified six areas to be addressed in bringing Charlotte to the realization of its international vision for the 21st century. These included:

- *Visibility and Awareness:* create a visible Charlotte through improved global and domestic awareness of Charlotte as an international city;
- *Community Services and Welcome:* develop an environment that welcomes and values international visitors and citizens and provide effective access to all necessary community services for international citizens, regardless of language skill or ethnic origin;
- *Education:* develop cultural understanding and tolerance in the Charlotte community and ensure that education teaches not only skills and languages but also history, geography and a sense of interconnectedness of the world today;
- *Higher Education and Business:* coordinate education and business to ensure an educated and trained workforce capable of meeting the demands of international business and manufacturing;
- *International Business and Economic Development:* support the present economic development focus of the city, county, Charlotte Chamber and Carolinas Partnership in encouraging and supporting both foreign investment in the region and the expansion of local industry through exports and investment abroad; and
- *International Organizations:* enhance the visibility, credibility and viability of Charlotte's non-profit international organizations and promote their effective coordination (City of Charlotte, 1994: 3-5).

While listing a number of both short and longer term measures to realize these objectives, the Plan did not detail the resources, action steps or legislation needed to turn them into reality. It was merely presented by the Mayor and the Cabinet as a recommended guide to future activities in these areas (City of Charlotte, 1994: 5-10). In short, the Strategic Plan did not commit anyone to do anything! This clearly suggested the very tenuous status of the Cabinet and its lack of independent resources or authority. To this point, the Cabinet was still a somewhat obscure entity and simply did not enjoy the kind of political support necessary to extend its mandate.

With the Strategic Plan in the public domain, the Cabinet now turned to the issue of implementation and its role in the process. At this point, there was even some question as to whether the Cabinet could continue in its current mode as the tenure of Pearson Fellow administrator was ending and no alternative arrangement was in the offing. This was resolved as the State Department, recognizing the importance of this endeavor, selected Charlotte as the first city to receive a second Fellow to oversee Cabinet operations. Action committees were formed to follow up on the priorities outlined in the Plan. Particularly effective were the efforts to coordinate local plans to promote Charlotte's involvement in the 1996 Atlanta Olympics and the creation of an extensive section of Charlotte's official home page on the internet ("Charlotte's Web") devoted exclusively to international resources, events, and contacts. The Cabinet was also beginning to gain attention elsewhere, as several communities (Columbia, S.C., Colorado Springs, Fort Worth and neighboring Gaston County) sought its advice (*Cabinet Minutes*, October 31 & December 12, 1994).

Still, little had been done to insure the permanence of the Cabinet or to secure broad-based political support within the community. It was still viewed as little more than one of the many boards used by the Mayor to advise him on the issues of the day. Convinced that the Cabinet had reached a critical turning point, the Mayor moved to strengthen its organizational structure. Formal criteria for membership were established, while terms were set and staggered for its thirty members. The Cabinet was constituted to "represent a broad spectrum of the community interests, reflect the growing diversity of the population and include individuals likely to be effective in carrying out the goals of the body" (*Cabinet Minutes*, October 31, 1994).

These changes suggested a greater sense of legitimacy and generated some new energy, as visitors and representatives of interested groups and organizations swelled attendance at subsequent Cabinet meetings to well over fifty. The Cabinet was beginning to emerge as a key player on Charlotte's international scene, which continued to expand through such initiatives as the addition of a Sister City in Ghana, a new export promotion program sponsored by the Chamber of Commerce, and an agreement to host the German track team as it made final preparations for the 1996 Olympics. The Cabinet's visibility was enhanced further by the publication of four editions of *World View* -- a newsletter publicizing matters affecting the city's international development (*Cabinet Minutes*, November 13, 1995).

The future of the Cabinet, however, still remained uncertain. The Pearson Fellowship expired and the administrative work was now being handled by an intern from one of the local colleges. Charlotte also elected a new Mayor, whose interest in matters international appeared limited. Presiding over his first Cabinet meeting, the Mayor raised pointed questions regarding its structure and functions and then appointed a committee to assess future prospects and opportunities (*Cabinet Minutes*, February 12, 1996). Some members even speculated that the Cabinet's days were numbered. The study committee, somewhat to the surprise of the Mayor, actually proposed a strengthening of the Cabinet. It recommended the appointing of a Board of Directors to provide the Mayor with direct guidance on specific issues or projects and the creation of a full-time Executive Director position (defined even more broadly as the city's International Affairs Director). These changes would certainly go a long way toward institutionalizing the Cabinet and elevating the importance of international concerns in general. An effort was to be launched to involve the City Council more directly in the work of the Cabinet to build the political support necessary to secure funding for the position (Mayor's International Committee, 1996).

The presentation of the report to the Cabinet elicited mixed reactions. The Mayor, as well as the majority of members, endorsed reform. However, the idea of a publicly funded Executive International Affairs Director generated considerable skepticism --

even in a room filled with committed internationalists. The proposal was submitted to the City Manager's Office as the first step in a process that would culminate in a formal request to the City Council for funding. The staff rejected funding of a full-time Executive Director. Instead, it proposed a rather modest $15,000 allocation for a part-time Cabinet administrator and the restructuring of the Cabinet into a non-profit 501(c)(3) corporation to permit additional private sector funding. This was similar to funding arrangements the city had concluded with other bodies over the years, including Charlotte Sister Cities. While recognizing the community's growing protocol needs (only some of which were international in nature), the staff recommended that they be met apart from the Cabinet (City Manager's Office, 1996). This was a considerable setback to those who sought to elevate the status of the Cabinet to a position atop a potential pyramid of local international organizations. The key was the proposed full-time Director post, which would raise the Cabinet's visibility and provide a single contact point for both the public and private sectors in addressing their international needs. While recognizing the importance of the city's expanding international agenda, only limited public funds were to be allocated to advance this agenda.

The Mayor embraced the City Manager's recommendations enthusiastically (*Cabinet Minutes*, February 3, 1997). While noting the unexpectedly large volume of internationally-related activity associated with his job, he seemed comfortable handling it on a more *ad hoc* basis and did not buy into the notion of an enhanced Cabinet-driven international superstructure. His efforts were useful in the successful "selling" of the revised proposal to the City Council. By mid 1997, the Cabinet had been restructured into a 501(c)(3) non-profit organization with a new five-person Board of Directors appointed by the Mayor to preside over the work of its standing committees. This was a most suitable arrangement for the mayor, whose enhanced relationship with the Board extended his international interests. The Cabinet became more representative and now included both private and public sector members. Some appointment powers were extended to the City Manager and the City Council to give them a political stake in the body. Finally, a part-time Executive Director was hired to provide ongoing leadership.

These measures have enabled the Cabinet to recapture some of the momentum lost during the preceding transition period. Recent meetings have been more substantive in nature; and the Mayor has appeared far more engaged and committed to acting through the body. The Executive Director has worked closely with the Board of Directors to build additional political support across the community. The standing committees are meeting regularly to further the goals of the Strategic Plan. Recent projects have included the Mayor's International Community Award to recognize the local contributions of international businesses, an initiative to encourage minority businesses to pursue foreign trade opportunities, an international education summit, the commissioning of a multi-lingual city promotional book, and cooperative planning with city officials to expand services to ethnic communities (*Cabinet Minutes*, 1997 and 1998).

Yet, at least to now, the drive to develop a distinctive "foreign policy" infrastructure in Charlotte has yielded mixed results. The role of the Cabinet remains modest even as it appears to have secured its niche -- at least for the time being. It has proven particularly instrumental in facilitating public-private sector dialogue and cooperation. No significant increase in public funding is anticipated; and the Cabinet's leadership has turned to external fund raising to help sustain its operations. This activity has been relatively successful but suggests the still tenuous nature of the enterprise. Volunteer efforts like those which have nurtured the Cabinet are essential. However, they do permit the city a relatively free ride in avoiding the level of expenditure commensurate with the requisite challenges of globalization.

CONCLUSION

The Mayor's International Cabinet of Charlotte has proven to be a particularly innovative body. It has supported many activities undertaken by the city as it has reached out to the world, while encouraging a series of steps in Charlotte itself to establish a more "global-friendly" environment. It has come to serve as an:

- *Advisory Panel for the Mayor,* setting priorities for issues to address;
- *Informational Clearinghouse,* promoting public awareness of international issues;
- *Facilitator and Implementor* of the Strategic Plan;
- *Coordinator* of an increasing number of international organization activities; and
- *Ceremonial Focal Point* for matters of an international nature

The successes of the Cabinet can be traced, in large measure, to the support it has generated from both public officials and the private sector. It remains dependent, however, on the relationship it is able to forge with individual mayors and its ability to secure sufficient financing to retain leadership and direction. Even as Charlotte's international involvements have grown and diversified, there is not -- as yet -- the level of political commitment necessary to guarantee a permanent role for the Cabinet within the city's governmental structure.

Institution building efforts such as this are somewhat problematic. It is difficult to sustain the enthusiasm and commitment so evident during the formative stages of organizations like the Cabinet, especially as existing political realities impinge upon activity. Municipal officials may be unwilling or unable to justify significant internationally-oriented expenditures when other more pressing local issues grab the attention of the electorate (Clark, 1996: 18). Producing relatively quick and tangible results may be critical to maintaining longer term support.

It is certainly premature to conclude that Charlotte, or other newly internationalizing cities for that matter, are engaging in their own foreign policies. For example, a recent survey found that city governments rarely take formal positions on foreign affairs issues and encounter little constituent pressure to do so (National League of Cities, 1997: 51). The increasing economic content of U.S. foreign policy, however, provides the impetus for urban paradiplomacy -- direct international activity transcending existing or traditional frameworks (Soldatos, 1989: 46).

New institutional arrangements are being crafted to facilitate these initiatives. Public-private partnerships are especially alluring, as they permit local officials greater latitude to act as entrepreneurs, strategists or even ambassadors in pursuit of the economic opportunities of globalization (Kim, 1995: 601). Steering clear of challenging or contradicting national policy, these efforts are beginning to assist a growing number of U.S. cities as they respond to the increasingly competitive pressures of the global economy.

REFERENCES

Abu-Lughod, J.L. 1995. "Comparing Chicago, New York and Los Angeles: Testing Some World Cities Hypotheses," pp. 171-191 in P.L. Knox and P.J. Taylor, Eds., *World Cities in a World System*. New York: Cambridge University Press.

Alger, C.F. 1988. "Perceiving, Analysing and Coping with the Local-Global Nexus." *International Social Science Journal* 117: 321-340.

Allen, F. 1996. *Atlanta Rising: The Invention of an International City 1946-1996*. Atlanta: Longstreet Press.

Bach, C.L. 1997. "U.S. International Transactions, Fourth Quarter and Year 1996." *Survey of Current Business*. April. p. 18.

Bilder, R.B. 1989. "The Role of States and Cities in Foreign Relations." *American Journal of International Law* 83: 821-831.

The Business Journal. 1992. August 24. p. 7.

Cabinet Minutes of Meetings. 1992-1998. Charlotte: Mayor's International Cabinet.

"Charlotte Becomes a Melting Pot." 1993. *The Leader* (Charlotte), June 18, pp. 1 & 28-29.

Charlotte Economic Development Department. 1992. *Four City Governments: International Organization*. Charlotte: Charlotte Economic Development Department.

Charlotte International Review. 1995. Charlotte: Atlantic Publication Group.

"Charlotte Logs Fastest Growth." 1994. *The Charlotte Observer*. July 15, pp. 1D-2D.

City Manager's Office. 1996. *Report on the Mayor's International Cabinet*. Charlotte: Office of the City Manager.

City of Charlotte. 1994. *International Strategic Plan*. Charlotte: Office of the Mayor.

Clark, T.N. 1996. "Does Globalization Limit Urban Leadership?" Paper presented at the Annual Conference of the Urban Affairs Association, New York.

Clarke, S.E. 1993. "The New Localism: Local Politics in a Global Era," pp. 1-21 in E.G. Goetz and S.E. Clarke, Eds., *The New Localism: Comparative Urban Politics in a Global Era*. Newbury Park, CA: Sage.

Clarke, S.E. and G.L. Gaile. 1997. "Local Politics in a Global Era: Thinking Locally, Acting Globally." *Annals of the American Academy of Political and Social Science* 551: 28-43.

Clearinghouse On State International Policies. 1992-1996. Chapel Hill, NC: Corporation for Enterprise Development, Newsletter of the State International Policy Network.

Cohn, T.H., D.E. Merrifield, and P.J. Smith. 1989. "North American Cities in an Interdependent World: Vancouver and Seattle as International Cities," pp. 73-117 in E.H. Fry, L.H. Radebaugh, and P. Soldatos, Eds., *The New International Cities Era: The Global Activities of North American Municipal Governments*. Provo, UT: David M. Kennedy Center for International Studies, Brigham Young University.

Crahan, M.E. and A. Vourvoulias-Bush. Eds. 1997. *The City and the World: New York's Global Future*. New York: Council on Foreign Relations.

Fry, E.H. 1991. "International Cities and the Global Political Economy." Paper presented at the 15th World Congress of the International Political Science Association, Buenos Aires.

Fry, E.H. 1993. "States in the International Economy: An American Overview," pp. 23-44 in D.M. Brown and E.H. Fry, Eds., *States and Provinces in the International Economy*. Berkeley: University of California, Institute of Government Studies Press.

Fry, E.H. 1998. "The Expanding Role of State and Local Governments in U.S. Foreign Affairs." Paper presented at the Annual Meeting of the American Political Science Association, Boston.

Fry, E.H., L.H. Radebaugh, and P. Soldatos. Eds. 1989. *The New International Cities Era: The Global Activities of North American Municipal Governments*. Provo, UT: David M. Kennedy Center for International Studies, Brigham Young University.

Goetz, E.G. and S.E. Clarke. Eds. 1993. *The New Localism: Comparative Urban Politics in a Global Era*. Newbury Park, CA: Sage.

Harris, N. 1997. "Cities in a Global Economy: Structural Change and Policy Reactions." *Urban Studies* 34: 1693-1703.

Hobbs, H.H. 1994. *City Hall Goes Abroad: The Foreign Policy of Local Politics*. Thousand Oaks, CA: Sage.

International Charlotte: A Guide to International Organizations and Activities in the Charlotte Area. 1994. Charlotte: Mayors's International Cabinet & International House.

Josephson, H. 1992. *Letters to Mayor Richard Vinroot*. Charlotte: April 20 & July 14.

Kim, P.S. 1995. "Foreign Direct Investment and the Role of Local Government: The Case of Hampton Roads in Virginia." *Urban Affairs Review* 30: 592-603.

Kincaid, J. 1989. "Rain Clouds Over Municipal Diplomacy: Dimensions and Possible Sources of Negative Public Opinion," pp. 223-247 in E.H. Fry, L.H. Radebaugh, and P. Soldatos, Eds., *The New International Cities Era: The Global Activities of North American Municipal Governments*. Provo, UT: David M. Kennedy Center for International Studies, Brigham Young University.

Knox, P.L. 1997. "Globalization and Urban Economic Change." *The Annals of the American Academy of Political and Social Science* 551: 17-27.

KPMG Peat Marwick LLP. 1994. *North Carolina 1994 Inbound Investment Study*. Charlotte: KPMG Peat Marwick LLP.

Mayor's International Cabinet. 1996. *Study Committee Report*. Charlotte: Office of the Mayor.

National League of Cities. 1997. *American Cities in the Global Economy: A Survey of Municipalities on Activities and Attitudes*. Washington, D.C.: National League of Cities, Research Report on America's Cities.

New York Times. 1996a. January 31. p. A1.

New York Times. 1996b. October 3. p. C2.

Peirce, N.R. 1993. "The Age of the Citystate." *Commentary*. Summer. pp. 4-9.

Rosenstrauch, L. 1995. Personal Interview. June 12.

Seattle Municipal Archives. 1985-86. *Record of the Office of International Affairs*. Seattle: Seattle Municipal Archives.

Shuman, M.H. 1986/87. "Dateline Main Street: Local Foreign Policies." *Foreign Policy* 65: 154-174.

Shuman, M.H. 1998. "Protecting the Local Globally." Paper presented at the Annual Meeting of the American Political Science Association, Boston.

Sister Cities International. 1996. *1996 Directory*. Alexandria, VA: Sister Cities International.

Soldatos, P. 1989. "Atlanta and Boston in the New International Cities Era: Does Age Matter?" pp. 37-72 in E.H. Fry, L.H. Radebaugh, and P. Soldatos, Eds., *The New International Cities Era: The Global Activities of North American Municipal Governments*. Provo, UT: David M. Kennedy Center for International Studies, Brigham Young University.

Stafford, W. 1997. Personal Interview. July 10. Seattle: Executive Director, Trade Development Alliance of Greater Seattle.

Walker, R. 1996. "Another Round of Globalization in San Francisco." *Urban Geography* 17: 60-94.

Wall Street Journal. 1996. October 25. p. A9A.

Yuthok, T. 1997. Personal Interview. July 10. Seattle: International Program Officer, Office of Intergovernmental Relations, City of Seattle.

Chapter 9

RECAPTURING THE FUTURE? THE IMPLICATIONS OF GLOBALIZATION FOR EDUCATION AND ENTREPRENEURSHIP IN U.S. ECONOMIC DEVELOPMENT STRATEGIES

Cal Clark, Johnny Green and Keenan Grenell

Globalization is clearly pushing the economy and society of the United States toward a profound transformation from the "Industrial Age" to the "Information Age." In particular, previously key industrial sectors are being forced "off shore" by international competition. Fortunately for America, they are being replaced by emerging new industries in the areas of high tech production, information and communications, and advanced services. The resulting economic change represents far more than just the replacement of one set of industries and jobs by another. Instead, the emerging fields of comparative or competitive advantage in the U.S. are quite different from the fading ones in terms of management, organization, and worker skills. Consequently, globalization is creating a much different economy and society. This transformation, in turn, strongly suggests that new economic development policies might be appropriate in such a radically changed environment.

This chapter argues that the old or conventional strategy of most states and localities, which are the principal practitioners of economic development policy in the U.S. due to the federal government's aversion toward "industrial policy" (Graham, 1992), is now outdated because of the new nature of competitive advantage in the United States. Traditionally, state and local governments have tried to lure new companies or to keep old ones from moving away by providing incentive packages in the form of tax abatements and subsidies which has been termed, perhaps somewhat disparagingly, "smoke-stack chasing." Such strategies, in essence, assumed that businesses would seek locations where their operating costs, particularly labor costs, would be minimized in what might be termed the "mass production" model. Now, however, it is precisely the industries that such a strategy sought to attract that are moving south across the Rio Grande and west across the Pacific at a rapid rate (Brace, 1993; Clark and Montjoy, 1998; Clarke and Gaile, 1998; Eisinger, 1988).

This seemingly should call for new economic development strategies since the old one is becoming increasingly obsolete. Here, we argue that state and local development strategies need to be reoriented to emphasize education and entrepreneurship. Ironically, these are two factors that spurred America's early industrialization in the late nineteenth and early twentieth centuries but that are now somewhat ignored by many practitioners of economic development policy. We begin by sketching how globalization is transforming America's "comparative advantage." We then argue that the "double E" strategy of education and entrepreneurship is becoming increasing vital for successful economic development. Finally, the conclusion points toward how this is creating a paradox for state-local development policy, as well as suggesting the need to transcend the normal cleavages between conservatives and liberals in American politics.

THE S-CURVE OF DEVELOPMENT: ECONOMIC CHANGE AND THE IMPACT OF GLOBALIZATION

Economic development is almost universally defined as growing wealth and prosperity as measured, for example, by GDP per capita. It is also commonplace to observe that such growth can only result from substantial and sustained increases in productivity or output per worker in a society. Thus, economic development is often considered to be almost (but not entirely) synonymous with industrialization because only mechanization can set off such a surge in productivity. The nature of industrialization itself, though, has changed dramatically over the 19th and 20th centuries in terms of what industry was the most advanced or "technological driver" -- first textiles, then iron and steel, then automobiles, and most recently high tech and advanced electronics.

Figure 9.1 sketches an overview of how these changes in leading industry constitute an "S-curve" in terms of increases in productivity and GNP -- the curve in Figure 9.1 is viewed (at least by economists) as looking like an S. In traditional agricultural economies, productivity increases are of necessity relatively small, but productivity and consequently GNP growth "take off" (Rostow, 1960) once industrialization starts. The first big jump is into light industry (e.g., textiles and shoes); and heavy industry creates another surge in productivity. Conventionally, it was assumed that the growth of the tertiary or service economy that succeeds heavy industry in this model would result in decelerating productivity gains and economic growth; and growth in the advanced industrial societies did indeed slow noticeably once they reached a "mature" level of development (Kuznets, 1976; Rostow, 1960). However, the recent surge in the high tech and information industries has led to the argument that these new technologies have generated a new upswing in productivity and growth (denoted by line #2 in Figure 9.1) that has been labeled the "new economy" (Atkinson, et. al., 2000; Friedman, 1999; Thurow, 1999).

Figure 9.1: Changes in Leading Economic Activity and the "S-Curve" of Productivity and GNP Growth

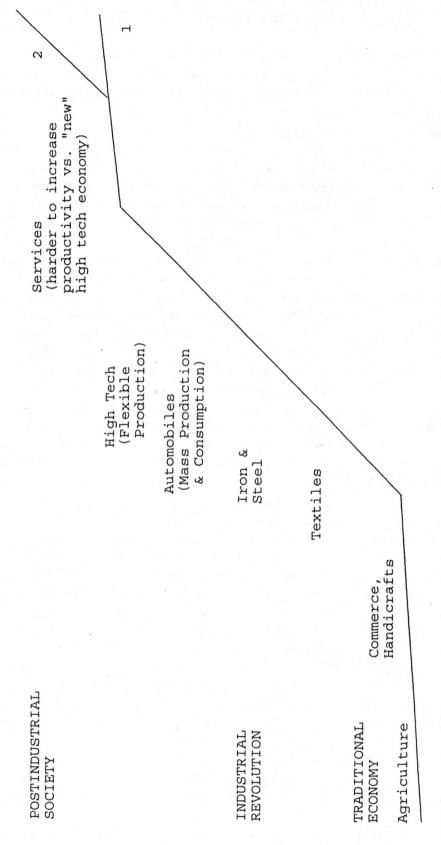

*Line signifies rate of annual GNP and productivity growth. Line #1 represents conventional theory; line #2 represents the theory of the "new economy."

The fundamental transformation of the world economy that has been termed "globalization" has had profound implications for how the industrial sequencing depicted in Figure 9.1 has influenced national economies. In essence, globalization refers to the growing economic interdependence (i.e., trade and capital flows and the activities of multinational corporations) across national borders that has marked the late twentieth century. Such interdependence, in turn, is the result of the transportation and communications revolutions of the second half of the century that made it possible to ship goods, funds, and information around the world cheaply and quickly. From this perspective, globalization is generally considered a process of the postwar era that "took off" in the early 1980s, although important aspects of it can be dated back to at least the 1960s (Gilpin, 1987; Greider, 1997; Thurow, 1992 & 1996).

This increasingly interdependent and complex global economy, furthermore, brought a marked shift in the geographic distribution of industry. Through the 1950s, industrialization had been limited to a small number of developed nations, primarily Western Europe, North America, and Japan; and these nations retained the full range of manufacturing industries from textiles and shoes to steel and automobiles. Lester Thurow (1992 & 1996) explains this in terms of the factors promoting industrialization. In this model, nations became rich and industrial during the 19th and first half of the 20th centuries by possessing and utilizing some combination of four resources: 1) natural resources (which could be sold or used as industrial inputs), 2) new technologies, 3) investment capital to put the raw materials and new technologies to work, and 4) human capital in the form of skilled labor and entrepreneurs. Except for natural resources, moreover, these resources were largely self-reinforcing (i.e., societies with the most advanced technologies, more capital, and a better educated population had a major advantage in reproducing these assets). Consequently, once a nation industrialized, it became very easy to retain its "comparative advantage" in manufacturing and industry.

Globalization, however, undercut all of these advantages except human capital, according to Thurow. Cheap transportation ended the advantage of having natural resources (e.g., the steel industries in Japan, South Korea, and Taiwan are now considered the most efficient and competitive in the world, although all three are resource poor); even most advanced technologies can be "reverse engineered" within a few years; and capital jumps around the world to the latest "hot spot" at the tap of a computer key, allowing almost any nation access to the investment necessary for industrialization

Beginning in the 1960s and accelerating in the 1980s, therefore, major economic sectors begin to move from the old industrial nations into what came to be called the newly industrializing countries (NICs), generally following the pattern of Figure 9.1 of first light industries and then heavy industries. To some extent, this represented the ability of NICs to obtain capital to buy standard technologies, but the key factor was the very low cost of labor in the developing world. The techniques of mass production that had been developed in the industrialized nations meant that only semi-skilled labor was necessary for many industrial operations. Before the revolution in transportation costs, industrial products had to be made and assembled near their ultimate markets, but as transportation costs dropped radically the semi-skilled work forces in the developing world became a viable option for producers of industrial goods destined for the developed world.

This set off a process that economists term "factor price equalization." The basic theorem of factor price equalization is that, all other things being equal, when two countries engage in trade, the price or cost of factors of production will become equalized between them. Thus, the increasing trade openness and radically declining transportation costs of the postwar era pushed industries and nations to compete (i.e., try to establish comparative advantage) based on minimizing labor costs. Consequently, wages for the same type of work converged internationally (Marshall, 1994; McMahon, 1988; Mokhtari and Rassekh, 1989; Thurow, 1992). For workers in the industrialized societies, the implications of factor price equalization in semi-skilled labor were extremely threatening. In essence, the price of labor was reduced to the level in the much poorer NICs (e.g., southern coastal China) which was truly far less than a "living wage" in the prosperous developed world. Consequently, as an industry (e.g., textiles and apparel) "matured" so that production became highly standardized and/or labor intensive, its production sites inevitably moved from the old industrial nations to the NICs (Gilpin, 1987; Thurow, 1992 & 1996).

As would be expected, these manifestations of globalization have been associated with profound changes in America's economy. The industrial drive that commenced after the Civil War soon made the U.S. one of the most competitive economies in the world, but by the 1970s the economy was clearly beset by declining productivity and competitiveness that produced growing concerns through the early 1990s. Over the last decade, in contrast, America's economy has clearly picked up again and is leading the world into new Information Age industries. Thus, the initial pessimism that a post industrial era might bring privation and poverty (represented by line #1 in Figure 9.1) is being replaced by optimism that the "new economy" will bring renewed productivity increases that will create the basis for continued (if not greater) prosperity (line #2 in Figure 9.1).

Figure 9.2 sketches the major structural factors affecting these transformations of the American economy since the late 19th century. This model suggests that the U.S. political economy has gone through three historical stages. First, America's highly individualistic culture generated new ideas which, when combined with opportunities from the environment, set off the "mass production" revolution under American leadership. Second, however, the long-term effects of the individualistic culture and the internal dynamics of largescale organizations led to institutional degeneration which was compounded by a changing environment for which the old forms of business and governmental organization became increasingly inappropriate. More recently, however, the dawn of the Information Age appears to be reinvigorating the economy and society of the United States.

Figure 9.2: Model of Evolving Business Competitiveness

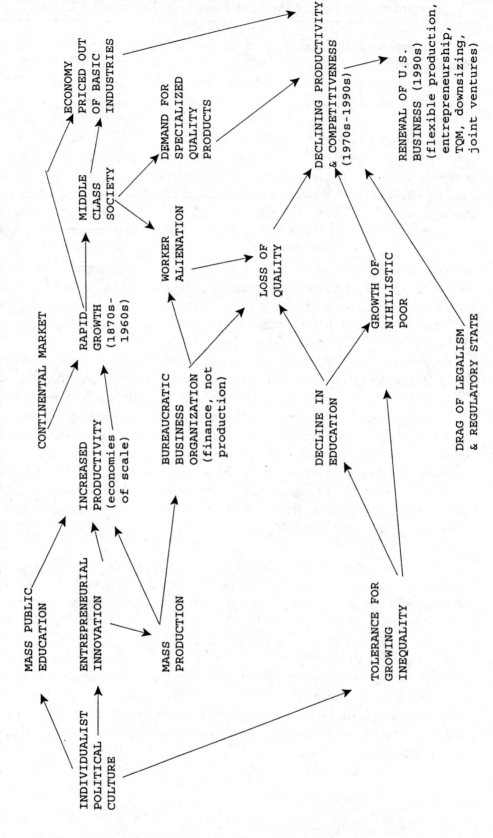

For business, mass production ("Fordism") represented an organizational revolution that transformed America's (and later the world's) economy and society. The tremendous increase in productivity meant that many goods became affordable for broad segments of the population; this combined with ultimately rising wages created a middle class society. Internally, the scale of production multiplied; and corporate entities became huge ("General Motorsism"), taking advantage of economies of scale, the development of professional management, horizontal and vertical integration, and the other advantages of large organizations (Chandler, 1977). Mass production also fit well with other aspects of America's political economy. An extremely rich natural resource base and a continental market fueled economic expansion; and the fact that America took a huge head start over the rest of the world in providing mass public education both created human capital for the rapidly expanding industrial workforce and hastened the advent of middle class society. More fundamentally, America's highly individualistic political culture supported both the program of mass education and the innovative entrepreneurship behind the U.S. industrial drive. Taken in its entirety, therefore, the top half of Figure 9.2 provides a thumbnail sketch of how America became arguably the most productive economy in the world early in the twentieth century and the world's "economic hegemon" for approximately three decades after World War II (Gilpin, 1987; Piore and Sabel, 1984; Reich, 1991).

Unfortunately, this system contained the "seeds of its own destruction." Large-scale business organizations tend to atrophy as entrepreneurs and engineers lose power to bureaucrats and finance officials (see Miller's, 1989, fanciful description of the corporate life cycle as moving "from barbarians to bureaucrats"). In addition, corporate organization, production line work, and the norms of middle class life in America interacted to produce growing worker alienation and loss of effort. The American political culture contributed to these dynamics as well. Individualism produced a tolerance for the growing inequality that resulted from American-style capitalism. This, in turn, helped undercut the educational system and exacerbated the growth of the "nihilistic poor" -- people who essentially "dropped out" of the economic and social systems because they had no hope of attaining the skills necessary to participate (West, 1993).

This general loss of corporate capability, moreover, was grievously exacerbated by changes in the economic environment. Domestically, the growth of the regulatory state added to the costs of businesses' own inefficiency. Externally, as sketched above, globalization brought increasing competition to many of America's leading industries. Moreover, the growing prosperity of the middle classes in the U.S. and elsewhere in the developed world created a growing demand for more specialized and high quality goods than America's system of mass production could turn out; and the advent of high tech industries put a new premium on "perpetual innovation" which was anathema to the large bureaucratic corporations that had dominated the American economy during the era of mass production (Birch, 1987; Kash, 1989; Piore and Sabel, 1984; Reich, 1991; Thurow, 1992 & 1996). This confluence of factors, then, brings us to the far right and almost the bottom of Figure 9.2 at the stage of the "declining productivity and competitiveness" of the early 1990s.

Fortunately for the United States, this did not represent the "end of history." Rather, American business began to "reinvent" itself by moving from mass production to "flexible production." This strategy, which was initially developed by the Japanese, involves using highly skilled and motivated workers (unlike the deskilled "drone workers" of mass production) to improve quality and flexibility. The focus is on making continuous improvements in production processes (e.g., making parts easier to assemble, reducing inventory) rather than on making dramatic product innovations (Harrison, 1994; Piore and Sabel, 1984; Thurow, 1992; Womack, et al., 1990). Flexible production requires skilled and autonomous employees, who are generally paid quite highly. Thus, it has been heralded as a management revolution that "reinvents" the corporation by transferring power downward and making even production work creative and rewarding. Many American corporations have, in fact, responded to competitiveness challenges by taking what Bennett Harrison (1994) calls the "high road" of flexible production, not just high tech firms like Motorola or Intel, but corporations, such as Proctor & Gamble and Rubbermaid, whose products seem quite pedestrian (Appelbaum and Batt, 1994; Collins and Porras, 1994; Harrison, 1994; Kanter, 1995; Kash, 1989; Rhinesmith, 1996; Smith, 1995; Waterman, 1994).

THE GROWING IMPORTANCE OF EDUCATION AND ENTREPRENEURSHIP FOR THE U.S. ECONOMY

The transformation of the U.S. economy from the mass production of the Industrial Age to the flexible production of the Information Age implies that both education and entrepreneurship will become increasingly vital for continued economic success and dynamism. Globalization and flexible production are forcing major changes in corporate structures. During the Industrial Age, huge vertically integrated corporations controlled vast markets and were operated by hierarchical command-and-control techniques internally. The intense competition and rapid push of globalization have made these bureaucratic behemoths too slow to be competitive -- witness the rapid rise of Microsoft at the expense of IBM (Carroll, 1993). Thus, *entrepreneurship* is becoming increasingly vital for business success.

The new Information Age industries and services are transforming the necessary characteristics and abilities of workers as well. Flexible production emphasizes worker autonomy and responsibility, product quality, and horizontal (as opposed to vertical) relations within the corporation, thereby requiring highly skilled and motivated employees. Konosuke Matsushita, late founder of the prestigious Japanese electronics company, felt that this transformation would work against the United States:

> We are going to win and the industrial west is going to lose. For you, the essence of management is getting ideas out of the heads of the bosses and into the hands of labor. For us the core of management is precisely the art of mobilizing and pulling together the intellectual resources of all employees in the service of the firm *(Financial Times, 1994)*.

The reason for Matsushita's confidence almost certainly rested not just on the Japanese managerial style, but also on Japan's educational system. As illustrated in Figure 9.3, flexible production requires well trained and highly skilled workers who continually learn and upgrade their skills. This obviously places a high premium upon *education*, where the Japanese system, especially for those not bound for college, is considered among the best in the world.

Figure 9.3: Shift In Needs For U.S. Work Force

Mass Production	Flexible Production
Emphasis on physical labor	Emphasis on innovation and discretion (mental work) even in physical tasks
Individual work	Team collaboration
Need for technical expertise	Need to "learn how to learn"
Slowly changing skill requirements	Constantly evolving skill requirements
Training for highly predictable work force	Training for highly flexible, learning work force

Source: Luke, Ventriss, Reed, and Reed. 1988. p. 148.

Education and entrepreneurship are key components of what is termed "human capital." Human capital has always been important for economic and social development. An overlooked argument in Adam Smith's *The Wealth of Nations* (1975) is that a critical part of a nation's wealth lies in its people. Ironically perhaps, many neoclassical economists who claim to be Smith's heirs conceive an economy as being based on the traditional "factors of production" --land, capital, and the undifferentiated supply of labor (Salamon, 1991), thus slighting Smith's key insight. A lack of concern with human capital, furthermore, would appear especially dangerous in the evolving age of globalization because, as argued in the previous section, the processes of globalization have severely undercut the importance of other determinants of economic success (i.e., the possession of capital, raw materials, and advanced technology), leaving human capital as the principal factor that differentiates the economic capabilities of various societies in today's world (Thurow, 1992).

Beyond the general importance of human capital, the advent of the Information Age has increased the importance of human capital for economic performance considerably. In fact, Michael Annison (1987: 328) concludes that human capital is now the key "transforming resource" that drives growth in advanced economies, such as America's:

The transforming resource may be thought of as what produces value in the society. In the industrial society, the transforming resource was processed energy... the generators... steam engines and power plants that made it possible to produce the automobiles, airplanes, televisions and products.... In the information society, the transforming resource has become "intelligence"... that allows us more effectively to develop products or services essential for our continuing success.

Thus, increasing importance is being placed upon what Peter Drucker (1989) terms "knowledge workers" and Robert Reich (1991) calls "symbolic analysts." More broadly, a variety of scholars are beginning to argue that human capital has become the key factor for a community's or nation's successful economic development (Clarke and Gaile, 1998; Salamon, 1991; Thurow, 1999).

Creating such a work force of necessity rests on revitalizing the system of mass education in the United States. As Lester Thurow (1992) argues, in industrial society, the current American educational strategy of providing a high quality education for the best 25% to 30% of students was quite successful because many occupations had become fairly de-skilled by mass production techniques. For the Information Age and flexible production, however, the key is providing a good education to the bottom half of the student population because they will determine how productive a society can be. It would seem quite ironic, incidentally, that American basic education has declined quite noticeably just at the time when a widespread consensus is emerging concerning the centrality of mass education and broad-based human capital developing for the continued vitality of advanced economies (Annison, 1987; Becker, 1992; Briggs, 1987; Hansen, 1988; Howell and Wolfe, 1991 & 1992; Kolberg and Smith, 1992; Marshall, 1994; Salamon, 1991; Smith, 1995; Thurow, 1992, 1996 & 1999).

This concern with improving education, it should be stressed, comes not just from liberals championing greater equity, but is also raised by pro-business conservatives who bemoan the low quality of workers. For example, listen to the perhaps surprising views on what affects U.S. competitiveness by Clyde Prestowitz (1988: 83), an official in the Reagan Department of Commerce whose major reputation was for advocating more aggressive policies toward Japan:

> Take Washington, D.C. Half -- that's right, half -- the children in our nation's capital will not graduate from high school. We are the only major nation that has had a decline in literacy in the past twenty years. At the national level we are effectively taking a quarter of our kids and throwing them on the scrapheap of history. The Japanese don't do that. The Germans don't do that, and neither do the Koreans or the Taiwanese or any other of our competitors. Ultimately, whether the United States can compete will be determined in the ghetto.

American, therefore, needs to improve the educational opportunities offered to a large minority of its youth, a cruelly ironic situation given the important role that mass education played in America's economic success in the late 19th and early 20th centuries (see Figure 9.2). As Kolberg and Smith (1992) discuss in *Rebuilding America's Workforce*, such a reform should have two central components: 1) school-to-work programs for teens and 2) continuous training for adults. A fundamental problem in American education is that the our public school system generally places students in two categories or informal tracks (i.e., college bound and non-college bound). Most school systems are designed to provide a strong education for those headed for college but, unfortunately, leave the non-college bound to find their own place in society and the world of employment (Kolberg and Smith, 1992; Smith, 1995).

Originally, public vocational education programs were designed to teach students a trade. They fell into disrepute, however, because stigmas developed that the people who took shop classes were somehow less intelligent. That attitude was coupled with a lack of effort on the part of school systems to tie the vocational training programs to specific industries and, in particular, jobs after high school. With only approximately 50% of high school students attending college (and even fewer completing college), common sense would dictate that America needs to refocus its efforts to provide much more relevant education. Such a task is clearly not impossible. One of America's largest employers hires non-college bound students and provides them with extensive technical training. While the U.S. military is probably not thought of very often as an educational success, it has a proven and impressive record in meeting one of our nation's most pressing needs at the dawn of the 21st century (Moskos and Butler, 1997).

In short, the transformation to an Information Age economy in the United States that is being accelerated by globalization is giving increasing importance to what might be called the "double E strategy" of entrepreneurship and education. This route begins with "hard work and hustling" on the edge of the business community to create the profits that are reinvested both in expanding the scope and scale of "mom and pop" businesses and in human capital development via promoting the education of the next generation who, in turn, tend to move into professional occupations. In the next stage, education and lifelong learning become vital for *both* the managerial and the production positions associated with flexible production -- small and high tech businesses that have to be highly entrepreneurial and have highly skilled and motivated employees (Birch, 1987; Butler, 1991; Drucker, 1989; Harrison, 1994; Thurow, 1996 & 1999).

This emphasis on education and entrepreneurship, for example, is the strategy that Asian Americans have practice *par excellence*. More surprisingly, perhaps, this also appears to be a "forgotten" strategy of African Americans. African Americans have always had a tradition of entrepreneurship and education which was quite vibrant even in the 19th century. African-American entrepreneurs existed in both the North and the South and provided community leadership. They respected and emphasized education; and, in fact, historically Black colleges in the South often provided better education than the more famous and better endowed state universities. Ironically, the victories of the Civil Rights Movement itself may have undermined this important tradition. With the end of segregation, money flowed out of the African-American community much more readily, thereby undercutting small Black businesses; many of the best and the brightest (and the most entrepreneurial) African Americans devoted themselves to political careers; and education probably deteriorated as well as many African American students lost empathetic and committed teachers in the public schools and as most historically Black universities and colleges lost much of their elan (Butler, 1991).

Overall, therefore, there seems to be a good foundation for a successful "double E" strategy in America's political economy. Historically, education and entrepreneurship played a key role in America's transition to an industrial society. The tradition appears strong among key new groups in American society, such as Asians, and even can be found in the ancestors of African-Americans who seemingly have been marginalized by the nation's contemporary market economy (Marable, 1983). The requisites for flexible production, consequently, can be found (probably in abundance) in American society. However, establishing a successful "double E" strategy will also necessitate a fundamental shift in economic development policy which, at least at present, is more problematic.

GLOBALIZATION'S PARADOX FOR ECONOMIC DEVELOPMENT POLICY

Globalization has set off a paradox for the economic development policies of states and communities in the United States. On the one hand, the rapid changes set off by globalization have enhanced the importance of economic development for subnational governments (Clark and Montjoy, 1998). On the other, the existing structures and principles of these policies almost certainly undercut America's ability to promote human capital development for flexible production, a presumed necessity for the nation's evolving comparative advantage. Continued economic development and the economic growth that it produces are key policy goals for states and local governments. Many states and local governments choose to design economic development programs around local laws and administrative procedures that tend to favor the "locational model" of economic development which is premised on reducing a firm's costs of production by providing tax breaks, free land, low interest loans, and cheap labor in order to entice companies to locate in the sponsoring state or local area.

Such a strategy, however, tends to overlook the centrality of human capital development for economic success. Studies have shown that human capital development provides the best opportunity for promoting long term economic growth (Bengtsson, 1991; Carnevale, 1992; Woo, 1991). This can be explained by the very logic of globalization. Firms are indeed relocating due to the restructuring economy and factor price equalization. However, those firms primarily interested in the lower production costs created by locational incentives are generally moving out of America altogether because of the much lower labor costs in developing nations. Thus, corporations that are most likely to be still interested in relocating within the U.S. are those that 1) use more technologically advanced production processes, 2) have more knowledge intensive service jobs (finance, medicine, computers, etc.), or 3) wish to move to existing high tech clusters. Moreover, because more highly educated populations earn more, human capital development should also ultimately increase local government revenues and probably decrease government expenditures for subsidized social services.

Consequently, state and local governments that are concerned and serious about long term, sustained economic growth would be well served by investing in human capital development programs. Yet, human capital development policies tend to be future oriented, contrasted with locational policies which tend to focus on strategies for improving current economic development. Unfortunately, "political" logic tends to be quite short-term, focusing upon re-election cycles of two or four years (Brace, 2001; Spindler and Forrester, 1993). Since many of the locational incentives are based on abatements in the very taxes that are used to fund education and human capital development, the paradox emerges that the economic development policies of many state and local governments appear to be counterproductive to the central goals these policies are supposed to serve!

Another major impediment to devising and implementing successful human capital development comes from the current gridlock in the battle between the conservative and liberal visions of where America should be going. From one perspective, this policy area might seem promising for overcoming the dominant ideological cleavage in U.S. politics today. This chapter has argued, in essence, that for economic development, a "liberal" means (improving human capital through a major educational effort) will almost inevitably be necessary if a "conservative" end (preserving business and economic vitality in the United States) is to be realized. Unfortunately, the political feasibility of meshing liberal and conservative approaches in education (or any other area) appears quite daunting.

Figure 9.4 illustrates this by providing a synopsis of the intersections and disjunctions between the two political philosophies on education. The first two rows suggest considerable complementarity (if not explicit agreement) between the two sides on "fixing the education mess." Liberals argue that public education provides an invaluable resource for allowing the poor to help themselves, one that is becoming increasingly essential for a middle class life as basic manufacturing in the U.S. falls victim to globalization. Conservatives, especially the business community, decry the declining competence (and even literacy) of American workers. Thus, both sides support improving education, albeit for different reasons. They also have different views of students which might or might not be complementary. Liberals argue that students need to develop self-esteem and motivation in order to be learn, while conservatives stress the support of families and the need for maintaining discipline in the schools. At the abstract level, these approaches would seem compatible since stronger families and better child self-images could well go together. In unfortunate reality, though, the debate over whether children need more cuddling or cudgeling still generates far more heat than light in many school districts.

Despite what should be a common interest between conservatives and liberals in bettering U.S. education, the actual gridlock in education policy is easily explained by the factors included in the bottom four rows. First, institutional features of the American education system explain why both liberals and conservatives face "cross pressures." While the business community may express a strong commitment to upgrading education, its strategy of procuring huge tax abatements to promote economic development undercuts educational finances (as noted in the last section). Likewise, the strong role of teachers' unions in backing the Democratic Party results in a loss of vigor in many liberal politician's willingness to challenge the educational *status quo*. Second, conservatives and liberals bring conflicting political values about how public services should be structured to the table of educational reform. Conservatives tout political decentralization and control by communities and parents, while liberals plead for a more centralized system since they believe that the federal government has the responsibility to ensure educational equality for all Americans.

Figure 9.4: Conservative And Liberal Disjunctions And Intersections On Education Policy

	CONSERVATIVES	LIBERALS
Complementary Values Supporting Better Education	Need for better trained workers	Provide basis for upward mobility by poor
Complementary (?) Insights about Students	Need for family support and discipline in schools	Children's self-esteem & motivation key
Institutional Blockage to Pushing Reform	Business demands tax abatements in primary source of education support	Support of teachers' unions and public control of education undercuts reform
Conflicting Political Values	Emphasize on decentralization and local community control	Belief in national responsibility for equal treatment of citizens
Conflict between "Theory" and "Practice"	Emphasis on vo-tech but aversion to public programs and primary concern with curriculum for college-bound	Emphasis on equal opportunity but opposition to "tracking" produces unequal results (schools oriented to college bound)
Conflict within Ideological Constituencies	Those who want calculus vs. those who want creationism	The "voucher wedge:" teachers' unions vs. many ghetto parents

Moreover, as the third row in the bottom section of Figure 5.4 indicates, both liberals and conservatives advocate positions whose actual implementation would probably be counterproductive to their proclaimed goals. Liberals argue that all children should be treated equally. In theory, this should mean that special attention should be attached to each child's educational needs and priorities. In practice, however, exactly the opposite results. Opposition to "tracking" students with different capabilities and interests means that most schools focus on the needs of the 30% - 50% of students who plan to go to college. In contrast, students with lesser ambitions and/or capabilities, the ones to whom liberal compassion should be directed, are left to look after themselves. Conservatives, for their part, are more supportive of business-oriented and vo-tech education in theory, but their aversion to high levels of public spending and their primary concern with their own, almost exclusively college-bound children results in few practical efforts to match the much better records of Germany and Japan in educating their future workers -- which obviously results in a competitive disadvantage for American industry (Smith, 1995).

Finally, both conservatives and liberals suffer from internal fault lines that limit the efficacy of their initiatives in the area of education. The conservative coalition contains a potentially uneasy alliance between the pro-business upper middle class and religious fundamentalists (Lowi, 1995). For education, this results in somewhat incompatible agendas -- which might be summarized as focused on, respectively, calculus and creationism. The liberal New Deal coalition had also become pretty tattered by the 1980s, if not earlier, because of the incompatible interests of various components (Lowi, 1979 & 1995). In the field of education, a new division has occurred in the last decade or so -- one that is quite ironic because it splits two of the few remaining elements among the liberals' core constituencies on an issue that had formerly bonded them together. Desegregation in the 1960s and 1970s stimulated a substantial amount of "white flight" to private schools. Especially after the decline in the quality of public education became undeniable, conservatives pushed for public support for private schools by providing "vouchers" for parents that their children could use at any school. Liberals vehemently retorted that this would destroy the public school system with especially deleterious results for the poor and minority communities who depend upon it -- that is, "savage inequalities" (Kozol, 1991) would escalate. By the 1990s, however, many parents in central cities saw vouchers as the only practical way to give their children a better education and protect them from gang harassment and enticements (Hill, et al., 1997). Needless to say (so we'll say it), such internal divisions among both liberals and conservatives can only promote gridlock.

Figure 9.4, therefore, suggests that the "intersections" between conservative and liberal goals for improving education have been submerged in the disjunctions between their political values and between important constituencies within each ideological school. This suggests that we can expect little change in the current system until different and more pragmatic approaches prevail. In short, the central role of human capital in economic development strongly suggests that America needs to "return to its roots" of emphasizing education and entrepreneurship. To "recapture the future by learning from the past," however, we must break down the prevailing stereotypes about possible policy packages and reconfigure economic development policy in a fairly radical manner.

REFERENCES

Annison, M.H. 1987. "New Economic Development." *Economic Development Quarterly* 1: 323-332.

Appelbaum, E. and R. Batt. 1994. *The New American Workplace: Transforming Work Systems in the United States*. Ithaca, NY: ILR Press.

Atkinson, R.D., R.H. Court, and J.M. Ward. 2000. *Technology, Innovation, and New Economy Project*. www.neweconomyindex.org.

Becker, G.S. 1992. "The Adam Smith Address: Education, Labor Force Quality, and the Economy." *Business Economics* 28: 7-12.

Bengtsson, J. 1991. "Human Resource Development: Education, Training and Labor Market Development." *Futures* 24: 1085-1106.

Birch, D.L. 1987. *Job Creation in America: How Our Smallest Companies Put the Most People to Work*. London: Macmillan.

Brace, P. 1993. *State Government and Economic Performance*. Baltimore: Johns Hopkins University Press.

Brace, P. 2001. "Mapping Economic Development Policy Change in the American States." *Policy Studies Review* 8:3.

Briggs, V.M. 1987. "Human Resource Development and the Formulation of National Economic Policy." *Journal Of Economic Issues* 21: 1207-1240.

Butler, J.S. 1991. *Entrepreneurship and Self-Help Among Black Americans: A Reconsideration of Race and Economics*. Albany: State University of New York Press.

Carnevale, A.P. 1991. *America and the New Economy: How New Competitive Standards are Radically Changing American Workplaces*. San Francisco, CA: Jossey-Bass.

Carroll, P. 1993. *Big Blues: The Unmaking of IBM*. New York: Crown.

Chandler, A.D., Jr. 1977 *The Visible Hand: The Managerial Revolution in American Business*. Cambridge: Harvard University Press.

Clark, C. and R. Montjoy. 1998. "Globalization and the Revitalization of U.S. Economic Competitiveness: Implications for Economic Development Policy," pp. 151-182 in K.T. Liou, Ed., *Handbook of Economic Development*. New York: Marcel Dekker.

Clarke, S.E. and G.L. Gaile. 1998. *The Work of Cities*. Minneapolis: University of Minnesota Press.

Collins, J.C. and J. Porras. 1994. *Built to Last: Successful Habits of Visionary Companies*. New York: HarperCollins.

Drucker, P.F. 1989. *The New Realities*. New York: Harper & Row.

Eisinger, P.K. 1988. *The Rise of the Entrepreneurial State: State and Local Economic Development Policy in the United States*. Madison: University of Wisconsin Press.

Financial Times. 1994. November 8.

Friedman, T.L. 1999. *The Lexus and the Olive Tree*. New York: Farrar, Strauss, Giroux.

Gilpin, R. 1987. *The Political Economy of International Relations*. Princeton: Princeton University Press.

Graham, O.L., Jr. 1992. *Losing Time: The Industrial Policy Debate*. Cambridge: Harvard University Press.

Greider, W. 1997. *One World, Ready or Not: The Manic Logic of Global Capitalism*. New York: Simon & Schuster.

Hansen, N. 1988. "Economic Development and Regional Heterogeneity: A Reconsideration of Regional Policy for the United States." *Economic Development Quarterly* 2: 107-118.

Harrison, B. 1994. *Lean and Mean: The Changing Landscape of Corporate Power in the Age of Flexibility*. New York: Basic Books.

Hill, P.T., L.C. Pierce, and J.W. Guthrie. 1997. *Reinventing Public Education: How Contracting Can Transform America's Schools*. Chicago: University of Chicago Press.

Howell, D.R. and E.N. Wolfe. 1991. "Trends In The Growth And Distribution Of Skills In The U.S. Workplace, 1960-1985." *Industrial and Labor Relations Review* 44: 486-502.

Howell, D.R. and E.N. Wolfe. 1992. "Technical Change and the Demand for Skills by US Industries." *Cambridge Journal of Economics* 16: 127-146.

Kanter, R.M. 1995. *World Class: Thriving Locally in the Global Economy*. New York: Simon & Schuster.

Kash, D.E. 1989. *Perpetual Innovation: The New World of Competition*. New York: Basic Books.

Kolberg, W.H. and F.C. Smith. 1992. "The Competitive Gap," in W.H. Kolberg, F.C. Smith, and C. Zigmund, Eds., *Rebuilding America's Workforce: Business Strategies to Close the Competitive Gap*. Homewood, IL: Irwin.

Kozol, J. 1991. *Savage Inequalities: Children in America's Schools*. New York: Crown.

Kuznets, S. 1976. *Modern Economic Growth: Rate, Structure, Spread*. New Haven: Yale University Press.

Lowi, T.J. 1979. *The End of Liberalism: The Second Republic of the United States*, 2nd Ed. New York: Norton.

Lowi, T.J. 1995. *The End of the Republican Era*. Norman: University of Oklahoma Press.

Luke, J.S., C. Ventriss, B.J. Reed, and C.M. Reed. 1988. *Managing Economic Development: A Guide to State and Local Leadership Strategies*. San Francisco: Jossey-Bass.

Marable, M. 1983. *How Capitalism Underdeveloped Black America*. Boston: South End Press.

Marshall, R. 1994. "Internationalization: Implications for Workers." *Journal of International Affairs* 48: 59-94.

McMahon, G. 1988. "Dual Factor Price Equalization: Elements of a Theory." *World Development* 16: 903-912.

Miller, L.M. 1989. *Barbarians to Bureaucrats: Corporate Life Cycle Strategies -- Lessons from the Rise and Fall of Civilizations*. New York: Potter.

Mokhtari, M. and F. Rassekh. 1989. "The Tendency Towards Factor Price Equalization among OECD Countries." *The Review of Economics and Statistics* 71: 636-642.

Moskos, C.C. and J.S. Butler 1997. *All That We Can Be: Black Leadership and Racial Integration the Army Way*. New York: Basic Books.

Piore, M.J. and C.F. Sabel. 1984. *The Second Industrial Divide: Possibilities for Prosperity*. New York: Basic Books.

Prestowitz, C.I., Jr. 1988. *Trading Places: How We Allowed Japan to Take the Lead*. New York: Basic Books.

Reich, R.B. 1991. *The Work of Nations: Preparing Ourselves for 21st-Century Capitalism*. New York: Knopf.

Rhinesmith, S.H. 1996. *A Manager's Guide to Globalization: Six Skills for Success in a Changing World*, 2nd Ed. Chicago: Richard D. Irwin.

Rostow, W.W. 1960. *The Stages of Economic Growth: A Non-Communist Manifesto*. Cambridge: Cambridge University Press.

Salamon, L.M. 1991. "Overview: Why Human Capital? Why Now?" in L.M. Salamon and D.W. Hornbeck, Eds., *Human Capital and America's Future*. Baltimore: John Hopkins University Press.

Smith, A. 1975. *The Wealth of Nations*. New York: Dutton.

Smith, H. 1995. *Rethinking America: A New Game Plan from the American Innovators: Schools, Business, People, Work*. New York: Random House.

Spindler, C. and J. Forrester. 1993. "Economic Development Policy: An Analysis of Two Models." *Urban Affairs Quarterly* 29: 28-53.

Thurow, L. 1992. *Head to Head: The Coming Battle Among Japan, Europe, and America*. New York: Warner.

Thurow, L.C. 1996. *The Future of Capitalism: How Today's Economic Forces Shape Tomorrow's World*. New York: Morrow.

Thurow, L.C. 1999. *Building Wealth: The New Rules for Individuals, Companies, and Nations in a Knowledge-Based Economy*. New York: HarperCollins.

Waterman, R.H., Jr. 1994. *What America Does Right: Lessons from Today's Most Admired Corporate Models*. New York: W.W. Norton.

West, C. 1993. *Race Matters*. Boston: Beacon Press.

Womack, J.P., D.T. Jones, and D. Roos. 1990. *The Machine that Changed the World: The Story of Lean Production*. New York: MacMillan.

Woo, J.H. 1991. "Education and Economic Growth in Taiwan: A Case of Successful Planning." *World Development* 19: 1029-1044.

Chapter 10

EXPORTING AMERICAN ECONOMIC DEVELOPMENT PRACTICE TO RUSSIA

Terry F. Buss

Part of the failure of US initiatives to build local/regional economic development capacity in Russia following the fall of Communism has been blamed on national factors, Russian culture, and American consultants. Much of the failure, however, probably resulted because American approaches to economic development -- highly successful in other contexts -- could not work during Russia's transition from a command economy to its current state. Such things as promoting entrepreneurship, developing public-private partnerships, creating a market economy, accessing start-up capital, attracting foreign investment, overcoming bureaucratic corruption and high taxation, working within the rule of law, and negating organized crime either should not have been done or could not have been done, leaving many of our programs ineffective.

In October, 1992, Congress passed the FREEDOM Support Act -- Freedom for Russia and Emerging Eurasian Democracies and Open Markets Support Act (P.L. 102-511) -- and offered other programs to help Russia make her transition from Communism to a democratic market economy (Tarnoff, 1998). The United States to date has invested a large share of $9 billion in grants and $8 billion in trade credits, trying to build Western-style economic development capacity in regions and localities across Russia (Tarnoff, 1998). Six years later, there have been many successes, but numerous efforts either failed outright or never lived up to expectations. Much of the failure can be laid at the doorstep of national politics, macro and fiscal policy, foreign affairs and the like. *However, some blame must attach to the incompatibility of American approaches to economic development -- highly successful in the U.S. and elsewhere -- but much less successful during Russia's transition.* The United States unwittingly tried to help in the wrong ways, at the wrong times, and in the wrong places. No one could have predicted how America's technical assistance effort should have been structured.

This chapter analyzes a variety of problems with our technical assistance effort which revolved around unanticipated peculiarities in the Russian transition that arose from radical differences between it and the American context for state-local development initiatives. The first part discusses failures in applying normal market logic to the Russian economy; and the second focuses on problems of political leadership in Russia. Finally, the conclusion asks whether the Russian deviations from the U.S. model have any implications for the current situation facing state and local development policy in the United States.

FAILURES IN U.S. MARKET LOGIC

It was generally assumed that the logic of U.S. market-based development could be directly transferred to the Russian economy. Yet, in a variety of important instances this was clearly not the case. This section describes several such false assumptions including: 1) the need to inculcate entrepreneurial norms, 2) the desirability of fostering business-government cooperation, 3) the desire of Russian business to convert to a market economy, and 4) the availability of start-up capital from either domestic sources or international investment. The analysis below is based on experiences in offering USIA programs in Russia during 1993-1997, along with interviews with program providers and participant observation in other programs.

American economic development practice promotes -- through training, technical assistance (TA), deregulation, and capital formation -- local entrepreneurship as a way to grow regional economies. Americans presumed that because Russians had no experience with market economies, having mostly worked for large, bureaucratic, monopolistic, state-owned enterprises or government, they would need help becoming entrepreneurial. Not so.

The Russians may be the most entrepreneurial people anywhere (Galuszka, 1993). Witness the explosion of small businesses across the country during the transition, started by people perceived to have no small business experience, capital, or knowledge of markets, under the most adverse business conditions anywhere (see below). In 1990, Russia went from total state ownership to 45,000 new private firms. By 1997, 842,000 firms had been established. Add to this an equal number of firms existing solely in the black market and the numbers are astounding (Tedstrom, 1998). Undoubtedly, Russians had to be entrepreneurial to survive under a Communist dictatorship. They bartered, worked the system, exploited the black market, and many prospered. Taking off their shackles allowed them to realize their full potential (Galuszka, 1993). Equally important, state-owned factories under Communism served as business incubators, or outright places of business, for vast numbers of Russian workers. Rather than toiling for the state, workers used state equipment and materials to manufacture products for sale on the black market (Kotkin, 1991). Fears about the absence of entrepreneurial spirit were unfounded. Russians generally did not need entrepreneurship training or technical assistance. Those who needed training may not have been viable prospects for entrepreneurship given business conditions Russians must endure.

In the U.S., much economic activity depends upon cooperation of the public and private sectors, often through public-private partnerships. Without a private sector under Communism, Russian leaders in public organizations and private business were expected to have difficulty coming together to pursue common goals. They would need help, it was presumed, forming the equivalents of our Private Industry Councils, Chambers of Commerce, Economic Development Corporations, and Regional Growth Associations.

Reality was just the opposite in Russia (Stoner-Weiss, 1997). For most industries of any size, entrepreneurs, managers and public officials are often the same people or associates of one another, wearing different hats as necessary. Industries under the old system were managed by party hacks; they were political, not economic entities. When industries privatized, these managers retained control of firms and stayed in business by partnering with public officials from whom they obtained favors -- government contracts, influence, subsidies, and protection. In exchange, government officials served on boards, received consulting contracts, or other benefits and side payments. I asked one Russian CEO whether the public and private sector was distinct. He said, "Definitely yes, but we keep moving the line between the two as it suits us." Helping Russians forge public-private partnerships was not only unnecessary, but probably legitimized public and private collusion.

Much economic development activity involves making firms more competitive in the market. Americans assumed that newly privatized Russian firms would want to become highly competitive so that managers and workers could prosper or at least survive. Quite the opposite was, and remains, the case. Many newly privatized firms were not economically viable, no matter how they were restructured, financed or developed. To stay in business, privatized firms retained as much of their socialist trappings as possible (Lieberman and Nellis, 1995). Under the old system, state-owned enterprises provided schooling, health care, dining facilities, recreation, and housing to workers. Under the new system, many provided unemployment benefits as well. Rather than trying to jettison these social services to government, many firms retained them, even though they drained away capital. Why? So that government would prop them up or risk turning out thousands of dependents (i.e., voters). Additionally, firms tried to retain monopolies in production, with government help, to improve their chances of survival. In the early days, firms classified as critical for defense were protected, so most firms argued that they were strategic, deserving continued state support. Russia has done little to convert its defense industry to civilian production and apparently uses it to help drive its economy through sales of technology and weapons to rogue states (EIU, 1998; Shlykov, 1997).

Because enterprises are not competitive, they have very little earning power. But they remain undeterred. They charge whatever they like for products; and when others will not buy them, they barter in exchange for things they want. They also take on huge debt by obtaining credit from other firms that they have no intention of paying back (Leitzel, et al., 1995). They in turn grant credit to other firms on the same terms. The *Russian Economic Barometer* monthly survey finds that 47% of business transactions are bartered (EIU, 1998). About 30% of GDP represents transactions in arrears. Two-thirds of all trade credits are overdue. A recent analysis by Brookings Institution researchers aptly refers to Russia as a "virtual economy" (Gaddy and Ickes, 1998). Forty-seven percent of

Russian enterprises reported losses in 1998. Eighty percent of firms privatized from 1993 to 1995 are expected to fail (Thornhill, 1998b). Ninety-six percent of privatized farms are bankrupt ("Russia's Farms," 1998).

Because firms have no earnings, they cannot pay wages. Workers often go for months and sometimes a year without pay. In one bank with which I was consulting, I inadvertently opened the wrong door. In a room with high ceilings, wood-paneled walls, and abundant gold leaf, there stood a pile of fish about four feet high on the marble floor. I was quickly ushered out by security. I found out later that the fish were bank employee wages, acquired from a fishing enterprise that could not repay a loan.

Americans were not prepared to deal with the absurdities left from central planning and the difficulties that these posed for development. One of these was location. In the U.S., economic development is driven by locational comparative advantages. Locational advantages are non-existent in many Russian regions, because industry was located for political and military reasons, not economic ones (Gaddy, 1996). Central planners located a factory producing hypodermic syringes on one end of the country and a factory producing needles on the other. Transportation costs for assembly, then shipment are exorbitant. Worse yet, the syringes do not fit the needles producing critical shortages. Foreigners often carry syringes with them to Russia because physicians tend to use the same needles on many different patients. What solution suggests itself for this problem? The vast majority of the Russian economy is doomed and not able to be saved no matter how dedicated the effort. It survives only through unpaid debt. Our projects expended considerable effort trying to resuscitate the terminally ill, while all but ignoring new ventures with potential.

Sooner or later, economic development comes down to capital. Entrepreneurs need capital to start and expand businesses. American economic development assumes viable capital markets, having only minor imperfections sometimes corrected by public intervention. A great deal of American practice concerns working with banks or financial institutions to improve access to capital, making it more available, lowering its cost, reducing risk, or improving terms. But Russian banks until very recently were not interested in lending, especially to small businesses. They profited through other means. Consider how the larger banks in Russia were formed and prospered (Mellow, 1997). First, they were capitalized by laundering money from black market activity and mafia operations (Thornhill, 1998a). Then, mostly through political influence and bribery, they received deposits from government agencies and state-owned firms on which they charged interest. Next, they began to participate in the privatization of state-owned enterprise, again through corrupt practices, such as using political influence to be appointed agents to facilitate privatization, eliminating competition seeking to acquire enterprises, and finally taking them over as part owners. Now, they are trying to take enterprises public on the stock exchange where they intend to raise even more capital. But they might all fail because they provided Russian Government Securities as collateral in borrowing from foreign banks. Thus, a large part of America's TA occurred without the essential ingredient -- capital. Without capital, very little could be done.

American economic development is driven in no small part by foreign investment. Russians and Americans focused much effort in attracting foreign investment, so far with limited success. Russians cannot understand why investors shy away. Since the fall of Communism, Russia has attracted only $10 to $12 billion or about $11 per capita annually in direct foreign investment, whereas Hungary with only 10 million people attracted between $2 to $5 billion or about $184 per capita annually (European Bank for Reconstruction & Development, 1997). As argued in the next section, bureaucratic corruption, absence of the rule of law, excess and arbitrary taxation, mafia control, and political instability (not to mention failure to institute economic and political reforms) explain the lack of investment by all but the few high-risk takers.

From an economic development perspective, though, the fact that Russians refused to invest in their own industries is telling. "Capital flight" -- transferring capital out of Russia to safe, often secret, bank accounts -- encapsulates the problem. Industry managers would sell products abroad, place receipts in special accounts, then transfer them out of country. Entrepreneurs and mafia leaders also transfer funds out. All told, as much as $20 billion a year could be leaving the country (Krayniy, 1997). So, $10 billion coming in, $20 billion going out. The European Bank for Reconstruction and Development estimates that 40% of Russian capital invested in Europe is from illegal sources. If Russians do not believe in their economy why should foreign investors? At any rate, American efforts to help capitalize businesses were difficult enough given the lack of finance available, but exporting what was available doomed many projects. Additionally, efforts at marketing regions -- many of which were professionally well done -- came to naught.

LEADERSHIP FAILURE

In addition to the problems of "market failure," Russia's poor quality of political leadership exacerbated the challenge of successfully promoting economic development. This section briefly considers two such problems of "government failure:" 1) the extremely high level of corruption and 2) the untoward side effects of leadership instability.

Americans coming to Russia knew about the corruption endemic in its system. It occurs in the United States as well, because stakes in economic development are high (in our system, apparently corruption takes the form of campaign contributions). The most debilitating instances of corruption from an economic development perspective occur when Russian entrepreneurs need permits to start or operate a business, become vulnerable to breaking laws, or pay taxes, especially customs. Depending on the business, an entrepreneur may need 15 to 20 permissions to proceed. At every stage, entrepreneurs can expect to pay handsomely first to have their application considered, then to have it favorably acted upon. Failure to pay can lead to delays literally in years and frequently to an ultimate denial of permission. A cottage industry of *fixers* has appeared in Russia: for a large fee, these entrepreneurs use political influence to obtain permissions. Managers and entrepreneurs claim that they spend 40% of their time on average dealing with government (Kaufmann, 1997). Russia ranks near the bottom on indices of political corruption, placing it along side Columbia and Nigeria (Mauro, 1997). Recently, 1,500 customs officials in Russia were indicted for corruption, as was the head of the national agency responsible for calculating taxes for businesses -- evidently he didn't.

American economic development succeeds under the rule of law. Americans knew that Russia had a long way to go in creating viable laws compatible with market economies. But they were not prepared for the instability that they found in the legal system. Russia's initial attempt at writing law related to economic development -- commercial codes, bankruptcy, land and property ownership, foreign investment -- was poorly done. This was to be expected. Russia had to reinvent itself from scratch; most countries take several hundred years to do this. What was problematic was that existing laws -- even though contradictory, counterproductive, and at best ambiguous -- were not uniformly enforced or not enforced at all, were not widely published or publicized, were often ignored, and were sometimes retroactive. In short, Russia had everything a legal system should not be. On the adjudication side, courts were highly political, prone to long delays, and not professionally run. In trying to engage in economic development assistance, Americans were never sure about the legality of their efforts or the prudence of their advice to Russians. In reality, Americans knew less about many issues than their Russian clients. For several years, it was not clear how to acquire land or buildings, enforce contracts, go bankrupt, or sue for damages, just to name a few.

Americans first working in Russia at the fall of Communism were not so much worried about mafia activity, but rather, bureaucratic corruption. As time passed, mafia activity began to stifle and then strangle economic development. The phrase mafia, in reality, stands for the sophisticated, organized crime operations, as well as unsophisticated, unorganized crime activity, both of which are violent, often indiscriminately so. Mafia activity affects economic development in several ways (Kreye, 1994; Meyer, 1998). The mafia imposes heavy fees on nearly all entrepreneurs for the right to do business. This drains profits that could be meaningfully spent in other ways, denies the government tax revenue by encouraging tax avoidance, and channels large sums of money into criminal activity. Much of mafia funds -- estimates range from $30 to $50 billion -- probably leave the country (Frazier, 1993). The mafia determines what kinds of businesses will survive and thrive, rather than markets. This substantially lowers economic efficiency. And mafia activity deters many prospective entrepreneurs from going into business. How bad is crime? In 1995, law enforcement was tracking 8,000 organized crime groups in Russia, 50 of which had international ties. About 40% of working capital in the entire economy was in cash, making it impossible to track. A recent study by the Center for Strategic and International Studies concludes that Russia is becoming a *criminal syndicalist state*, that is, a partnership of bureaucrats, politicians and mafia leaders (Meyer, 1998; Nemtsov, 1997).

In the American political system, leadership changes at the city, state and national level can mean reversal or termination of economic development initiatives, but for the most part, change in our system tends to be incremental and moderate. In Russia, leadership change was all too prevalent. President Yeltsin originally appointed all of Russia's 89 regional governors. Depending on their subsequent politics, he fired many of them. Then he allowed some to be elected. In many regions, governors changed three times in five years. In some regions this meant 180 degree, then 360 degree, reversals:

democratic reformers replaced by Communists, replaced by opportunists. Americans working on Russian economic development, especially at the *oblast* level, soon found that frequent leadership changes either terminated projects, completely redefined them, or forced them to start over. Americans were never sure with whom they would be working over the course of their projects. If new governors did not support past gubernatorial efforts, then efforts were wasted. Moreover, these problems are exacerbated by the extreme independence of regional governors in Russia. In some regions, strong governors withhold taxes from Moscow, refuse to implement laws they don't like, and harass representatives from the national government (Kirkow, 1995).

In American economic development, technical assistance is widely available; and those in need compete for it. Sometimes they succeed. In Russia, it was often the case that Americans had to provide incentives to Russian officials to get them to accept help. This took several forms. In order to get the right people to the U.S. for training, some of the wrong people had to be sent as well. The U.S. liked to send young reformers on its visitors programs, but often had to send old party hacks as well. Another strategy was that Americans were required to hire Russian partners, rather than the Russian partners contributing their own resources. Both exigencies reduced scarce resources and jeopardized project objectives.

LESSONS FOR U.S. ECONOMIC DEVELOPMENT POLICY

As other chapters in this book demonstrate, the forces of globalization are pressing major changes on the United States economy and political system at all levels. Failures that our conventional assumptions about development caused in providing technical assistance to Russia, therefore, could prove instructive at home. Perhaps the most instructive lesson is that the political and economic leadership and citizenry must *share a common set of values and beliefs* in general about how economic development will occur. Without these shared values, conflict, confrontation, and destructive self-interest will take over. This point was brought home recently in Seattle at the World Trade Organization's trade negotiation meeting. Imposing trade, environmental, labor, and development on countries will not work unless those affected buy in to the process and results. Globalization, at least in its formative stages, appears to open up more cracks than it seals.

The Russian experience points up dramatically the *folly in trying to re-engineer entire economies* to achieve development and political goals. Economic development is an incremental process that creeps along. "Silver bullets" just do not work. Economies and political systems cannot handle them. President Clinton's New Markets Initiative to attract billions into distressed areas, the National Council for Sustainable Development to address environmental and economic problems, and Empowerment Zones to turn around distressed communities are great ideas, but they fail to take into account how development actually occurs -- slowly. After all, the Appalachia Regional Commission, Economic Development Administration, Department of Housing and Urban

Development, and Tennessee Valley Authority have poured hundreds of billions into similar projects in many cases with little effect.

The Russian experience emphasizes the importance of *building on the existing strengths* of economies and political systems, rather than trying to change them into something else. To be competitive in the global economy, every city and state wants to become the next Silicon Valley, endowed with unlimited venture capital and boundless entrepreneurship. Cities and states are willing to spend lavishly to achieve this. But world class global competitors are that way because they possess irreplaceable comparative advantages out of the reach of others. Cambridge, Massachusetts is the undisputed capital of biotech entrepreneurship because of MIT and a cluster of world-class research companies. Efforts to clone MIT and its cluster of firms wastes resources that could have been profitably invested in other ways.

Finally, Russia calls into question the wisdom of allowing economic development to be predominately the province of the state. Public officials in the U.S. can *set goals, marshal resources, promote stability, and cheer lead for economic development*, but they should never be responsible for it wholesale. We tend to forget our history in economic development when government participated too heavily. Much of the Robber Baron activities 100 years ago occurred because of the collusion of government and entrepreneurs, a situation parallel to contemporary Russia. Public-private partnerships are a better way to go as long as their activities are transparent and inclusive. But real development only occurs because private investors and entrepreneurs have confidence in economies and political systems.

REFERENCES

Economic Intelligence Unit (EIU). 1998. *Russia: Country Report, 1998*. London: The Economist.

European Bank for Reconstruction & Development. 1997. "Russian Federation Presentation." *Transition Report Update*, April, p. 12.

Fraser, H. 1993. "Milking Mother Russia." *International Management* 48: 46-47.

Gaddy, C.G. 1996. *The Price of the Past*. Washington, D.C.: Brookings.

Gaddy, C.G. and B.W. Ickes. 1998. "Russia's Virtual Economy." *Foreign Affairs* 77: 53-67.

Galuszka, P. 1993. "When the Shackles Come Off." *Business Week*. 1993 Special Enterprise Issue. p. 76.

Kaufmann, D. 1997. "Corruption: The Facts, Foreign Policy." *Financial Times*, September 16.

Kirkow, P. 1995. "Regional Warlordism in Russia." *Europe-Asia Studies* 47: 923-947.

Kotkin, S. 1991. *Steeltown, USSR*. Los Angeles: University of California Press.

Krayniy, V. 1997. "Come Back All is Forgiven." *Interfax AIF*. July 14-20.

Kreye, A. 1994. "Mafia Capitalism in Moscow." www.users.interport.net.

Leitzel, J., C. Gaddy, and M. Alexeev. 1995. "Mafiosi and *Matrioshki*." *The Brookings Review* 14: 26-29.

Lieberman, I.W. and J. Nellis. 1995. *Russia: Creating Private Enterprises and Efficient Markets*. Washington, D.C.: World Bank, paper #15.

Mauro, P. 1997. "The Effects of Corruption on Growth, Investment and Government Expenditure," in K.A. Elliott, Ed., *Corruption and the Global Economy*. Washington, D.C.: Institute for International Economics.

Mellow, C. 1997. "Russia's Robber Barons." *Fortune* 135 (March 3): 120-125.

Meyer, C. 1998. "Limited Rules of Discourse," *Washington Times*, July 31.

Nemtsov, B. 1997. "Enough of Building Gangster-Style Capitalism," *Komsomolskaya Pravda*, July 29.

"Russia's Farms." 1998. *The Economist*, July 25, p. 50.

Shlykov, V. 1997. "The Political Economy of Russian Defense." Paper presented at the U.S. Naval Postgraduate School, Monterey, California.

Stoner-Weiss, K. 1997. *Local Heroes: The Political Economy of Russian Regional Governance*. Princeton: Princeton University Press.

Tarnoff, C. 1998. *U.S. Assistance to the Soviet Union and Its Successor States*. Washington, D.C.: Congressional Research Service, Library of Congress, 98-43F.

Tedstrom, J. 1998. *Estimating Russia's Informal Economy*. Santa Monica, CA: Rand Corporation.

Thornhill, J. 1998a. "Cronyism Doubts Surround Plan to Protect Ailing Banks," *Financial Times*, August 20.

Thornhill, J. 1998b. "Investors Question Whether Russia has Strength to Bear Financial Crisis," *Financial Times*, July 30, p. 5.

INDEX